THE
CREATIVE
LEADER

Who Said Creatives Couldn't Be Bosses?!

Antwain Jackson

THE
CREATIVE
LEADER

Who Said Creatives Couldn't Be Bosses?!

Antwain Jackson

The Creative Leader
Who Said Creatives Couldn't Be Bosses?!
by Antwain Jackson

© 2020, Antwain Jackson
info@antwainjackson.org

Published by Anointed Fire

Cover Design by J. L. Designs Creative Group
Photography by Edward Rhone
Edited by Anointed Fire

ISBN: 978-1-7331127-6-5

Acknowledgments

Kirk Emile Jackson
Rest well, Dad!
I hope you're leaning over the balcony of Heaven, cheering me on.

Janet Ware
Love you, Mom!
I realize the reason I don't give up is because I got my fight from you!

My Hero: James A. Stewart
Besides Jesus, there is no other man on this planet who's formed me greater than you.
You are my gift from God.

Dr. Myles Munroe
Your teachings set me free from religious thinking.
They will hear you in this book and I have no problem with that!

Aignee & Sydnee
You two are my reason.
You both make me a better man just being your Father.

Table of Contents

Foreword...IX

Introduction...XI

Leadership + Creative...1

The Jordan Effect...15

    Your Belief System...19

    Self Discipline...22

    The Benefits of Discipline.....................................25

    Managing Your Thought Life...................................28

You Have Big Eyes (Vision) 33

Maturing as a Leader..47

    Unrealistic Expectations..49

    Misrepresentation...54

    Procrastination...58

    True Representation...61

    Maturing as a Leader...63

Leadership Beliefs..69

Maturing in Your Personal Beliefs...........................93

Your Worldview...109

How to Become a Valuable Leader..........................129

The Way Up is Down...147

The Creative Leader..161

    Let's Go to Church...170

    Let's Go to Work..174

    Let's Get to You..176

    Let's Get to Others...179

    Your Leadership Unlocked......................................181

Foreword

If anyone in any corporation or team wanted to build momentum and morale, their first conversation is most likely going to be with the creative department of said company.

Anytime I've seen great momentum and positive energy around a certain cause or vision, it's almost certain that the creative fuel had been maximized. Yet, there always seems to be a struggle between creatives and logistics people. A lot of creative leaders seem to lack administrative leadership— and administrative leaders seem to quarrel with creatives.

In this book, my friend, Antwain, will bridge that gap and explain the value of the creative and how to work towards building those strengths. He is one of the most qualified people I know firsthand to speak to this.

First of all, I have yet to meet someone who cares as deeply as he does, regardless of his role in it. I've seen him flourish as a logistics person and I've seen him flourish as a creative leader as well. I've said this many times while leading my own business and movements:
1. You cannot pay people to CARE.
2. Service is a choice.

I love the way he has cared for my causes and made them his own. I would strongly suggest you read this book with an open heart. You can have confidence that Antwain knows what he is talking about; this is why he made the choice to serve the readers of this book, and he does this with great care. I believe that if you will read and apply what's in this book, your creativity will go to a greater dimension, and therefore, your team, your company and your mission will find itself in a much more effective zone.

Israel Houghton
Grammy Award Winner

Introduction

Why write another book on leadership? Leadership, in my opinion, is a crucial component in achieving goals and aspirations. It is the only way to see dreams fulfilled. As complex as leadership is, it is also one of the simplest functions to perform if certain disciplines are adhered to. Leadership isn't a task, it's a person. It's YOU! Leadership is you discovering you, understanding you, and leading you in such a way that other people desire and trust you with their lives. Dr. Myles Munroe said, "Everyone is born a leader, but most will die followers." It takes discipline to produce the fruit of gifted leadership in one's life.

My second reason for writing this book is because I believe the conversation about leadership needs a fresh perspective. Leadership has been sold in lofty ideals, and these ideas or concepts have made it unattainable for the regular Joe's like you and I. I am a simple person who didn't grow up with a silver spoon anywhere near my mouth. This book is for the people who know that there is great potential in their lives, but needs to hear it from someone who is like them. I'm your guy! This book will be simple, practical, fun, real, and full of the wisdom you need to help you in your quest to innovate your leadership.

A significant piece of my life leadership journey has been uncovered and fine-tuned through my service to the church. Leadership was for the selected few, and the qualifications were somewhat ambiguous. You have to understand, I was raised in an environment that was very traditional, robotic, very heavenly-minded and not creative. There was no need for personal development because, after all, the whole goal was Heaven, right?! If you're not into the "religious stuff," don't put the book down yet. I'm using my experiences in and with the church to show you the ability to even innovate an institution that is as old as they come. However, I've seen significant innovations in its expression and approach. I've come to realize that church isn't a service, but a mission.

In this practical and powerful guide, I'm going to help you to understand what it means to be a leader and how to impact the world with your leadership and your creativity. See you at the TOP!

Leadership + Creative

There has been a lot of discussion surrounding leaders and leadership, and this conversation has been going on since the beginning of time. Over the years, we've seen corruption, assassinations, tyranny and people usurping authority because everyone believes that they have what it takes to be a great leader. Talk shows are burning up the airwaves because both believers and non-believers alike are hungry for information. Everyone is looking for solutions to the many problems we face, but not everyone is willing to be a solutionist. We have an overflow of takers in this world, but not enough givers. This has caused an imbalance in our economic system, and anytime a community, an organization, a family or a country is imbalanced, faulty leaders will suddenly rise up and attempt to fix whatever it is that appears to be broken. Nevertheless, a great and functional leader is a disciplined individual who's overcome a host of problems on a personal level and has now risen up to help others overcome those issues, either individually or corporately. This means that a true leader must have discipline; this is how we can differentiate a faulty leader from a functional one.

The root word of "discipline" is "disciple." What is a disciple? After all, this word does have some religious undertones to it, but a disciple, in short, is a follower of a person or a concept. Cambridge Dictionary defines the word this way: "a person who believes in the ideas of a leader, esp. a religious or political one, and tries to live according to those ideas." Look around you. There is nothing in this Earth that hasn't been touched by the hands or the concepts of a human. This means that we are all followers of someone, whether we know that person or not. Every leader is a follower, even if that leader isn't currently following another human; instead, he or she may be following a set of beliefs and principles that were instituted by someone who died hundreds, if not thousands, of year ago. Nevertheless, we all need leaders if we are going to be pioneers. If we want to change this world, we have to understand that we cannot do it alone. We need principled and disciplined people to rise up and submit to the leadership and the correction of other human beings, after all, we submit to one another. The highest-ranking officials among us understand this concept. All of our Presidents were always surrounded by advisors. Most, if not all, wealthy people have many mentors in the form of financial advisors, accountants, PR agents, attorneys, stockbrokers, etc. Most corrupt leaders who have risen to power either had no one advising them or they had what we commonly refer to as "yes men." These are people who tell their leaders and their friends what they want to hear out of fear of being rejected, and in some instances, persecuted or killed. We commonly refer to these types of people as enablers. And if you pay close attention to the celebrity world, both current and past, you'll see a pattern of great minds who have either lost their minds or their lives because they'd surrounded themselves with enablers. This is why every great man or woman needs to be disciplined and needs to surround themselves with disciplined people. And then, of course, every disciplined person needs to create space in his or her life to disciple someone else.

Leadership, to me, is a simple concept. Leadership is the discipline that a person has to lead themselves to a desired destination that influences and teaches other people that they have the potential to take themselves to the destination that they have planned for their lives. Oftentimes, people think that leadership is emulating a person. It isn't. You're simply learning the discipline that another person has so that you can learn to discipline yourself. You're not supposed to emulate me, you're supposed to follow me—there's a big difference in the two, and as long as we don't grasp this concept, we'll keep throwing away or burying our own identities in our attempts to fix what we believe to be wrong in our lives. Every problem that you are facing today has everything to do with this very underestimated and rarely used word—that's discipline, of course. If you are ever going to be a great and functional leader, you have to first find some undisciplined areas in your life and discipline yourself in those areas. If you don't eat healthy, you need to start eating healthy, if you don't go to the gym, you need to start going to the gym, if you don't get along with people, you need to learn to get along with people. Discipline is all about knowledge. Some people were never taught to eat right, exercise regularly or have healthy relationships. Nevertheless, we can't keep using our parents' failure to teach us or their lack of discipline as an excuse to remain mediocre. There are people out there who will always live beneath their standards if you and I don't get ourselves together and take our places in leadership. But before we go any further, let's define the word "leader."

A leader is a disciplined person or, better yet, a faithful disciple. That's short and to the point, of course, but there's much more to this. A leader is a person who has successfully overcome his or her own limitations, and is now teaching others to do the same. Harriet Tubman is a great example of a leader because she escaped slavery, and she didn't just relish in her own freedom, but she went back to rescue others and lead them out of slavery. She found herself in a bad place, but she chose to not remain there. You see, here's the thing about wrongful thinking—as bad as it is, it still provides its citizens with a level of comfort. Notice I used the word "citizens" so that you could understand that a wrongful way of thinking is more than just bad ideas; it's a country within its own rites, filled with citizens, laws and governors. This is why toxic people tend to attract and are attracted to other toxic people. With that said, Harriet Tubman overcame a lot of hardships that are not necessarily mentioned in our history books. She had been struck in the head with a two-pound weight while she was still a slave. This caused a brain injury, and because of this injury, Mrs. Tubman was known to fall asleep mid-sentence; she would go into a deep slumber, and would suddenly arise from that slumber and go about doing what she had been doing before she fell asleep. She also suffered, as a result of this attack, from severe headaches and seizures. Nevertheless, she didn't allow this to cripple her perspective. She wanted to be free and she would have her freedom. And she decided that freedom wasn't just for her; she wanted every Black man and woman to enjoy the freedom that the North offered African-Americans. We all know the story. She successfully ran away and got her freedom. After this, she returned to the South on several occasions, helping to free other slaves.

Howbeit, Harriet Tubman faced another issue—an issue that other leaders are often surprised to come across. She met African-American men and women who did not want to be free. In other words, they didn't want a mentor. Sure, they didn't like being slaves, but they didn't want to take the risks involved with trying to escape. If that wasn't scary enough, they definitely didn't want to face the uncertainty of living in a new state, surrounded by a bunch of unfamiliar places and faces. So, they chose to remain in slavery, meaning, they didn't just make this choice for themselves. They also made this choice for their children and the future generations to come. Nevertheless, Harriet got over the shock of it all and continued to lead the ones who wanted to be free to freedom. This is essentially what you and I will be doing. We are creatives; we are leaders. What we do is find a problem, and then, we set out to solve it. But we don't do this by talking about the problems; true leaders list and test solutions. Of course, every problem has to be met with a strategy. When Harriet Tubman decided to free herself, she had to develop a strategy. She had to know which direction to run in, when to leave and the problems she would face while attempting to get to her destination.

Every leader needs a strategy. In every world or market, the word "strategy" has a different undertone. For example, a strategy used by military officials in times of war is called a war tactic. A strategy used in the business world is called a business plan. A strategy used in family matters is called counseling. The strategy that bridges all of these worlds together is called creativity. *A strategy is a plan to approach a problem.* Every system, organization or man-made establishment has problems, but these problems are not a death sentence to the structure; they are opportunities for the system, the organization or the establishment to grow and to flourish. Nevertheless, only leaders will see the potential of a mess; everyone else will just spectate and complain. Every idea is a response to a problem, but of course, only leaders implement and execute those ideas, and they do this consistently. Take a look at the Leaders' Spectrum below.

Consumers/ Complainers	Spectators/ Procrastinators	Producers/ Solutionists/Doers

Make no mistake about it, every person on this spectrum is a leader, but not everyone is leading people in the right direction. Imagine a group of people at a town hall meeting, and the complainers are doing what they do best— highlighting problems. This is how they lead. Every leader will always inspire the people who are like them, so at this meeting, you'll notice that people who are like-minded will cheer the complainer on. They will even draw enough inspiration from the complainer to encourage them to get up and share their own grievances. Also, another group of people will be found in this crowd; this is going to be your majority or your spectators. Spectators have opinions, but they are too afraid to voice their opinions because they fear that their suggestions will be rejected or worse, that they'll end up being humiliated. So, spectators will sit quietly in the meeting, and many of them will pick a side based on the temperature of the meeting. If it appears that the complainers are winning, most spectators will lean towards the side of the complainer. If the producers are winning, most spectators will lean towards the side of the producer. These are the people who will catch you alone after the meeting and say that they agree with you; they will also catch someone who opposed your views and tell that person that they agree with him or her. Spectators can be provoked to speak if someone who is a known spectator suddenly speaks out. In other words, they are unstable followers, but the great news is, they are further along than the complainers. This means that there has been some movement or growth in their lives, since we all start off as consumers. And finally, there are the producers or solutionists. These are the people who sit in the meetings and come up with strategies and solutions to all of the problems that are introduced; these are the true leaders. Solutionists are people who've tapped into their creativity; they are the people who see problems and get excited because those problems, to them, represent another opportunity for them to exercise their creative muscles. It's important for you to know the people on this spectrum, because you are going to lead them all. As a leader, you have to learn to identify your complainers, your spectators and your solutionists. This is the mark of great leadership. Plus, it allows you to maximize your own creativity as a leader by knowing who to put in place at any given time. For example, in basketball, a coach is not going to send his weakest player on the court if there are just a few minutes left in the game. By knowing who his all-stars are, a coach can lead his team to victory consistently by strategically using every player on his team. He places spectators on the bench, he places some complainers in the game, but he commands them to give the ball to the solutionists. Now get this—all of the guys can play basketball, but a good coach doesn't measure skill, he measures competence.

Again, every leader needs a strategy—that strategy is called creativity. Creativity is the ability to create. This is, at least, Merriam Webster's definition of the word. My definition of creativity is when one's ability to create is met by maturity, discipline and a vision. Of course, there are levels of creativity. For example, some people create solutions, while others create beautiful or palatable solutions. Think about a company that produces medicine. Some companies are only focused on producing medicines that work. While this is great, they don't put much effort into the visual presentation, nor do they attempt to mask the taste of the chemicals that they are selling. Their products are oftentimes very effective, but they don't necessarily maximize their own potential because they want to save money. However, some companies come out with medicines that aren't as effective as the aforementioned companies. Their products do the jobs they claim to do, but for short periods of time. They get more sales and more attention because they put the time, money and the effort needed to created visually attractive meds that have a more palatable texture and aren't so bad on the taste buds. In other words, they put more time into creating a strategy than their competitors. Two companies can have the same budget—one company may put more money and manpower into creating an effective product, but the other company may balance their budget, spending half the time and energy producing the product as their competitor, and the other half of their time and energy is invested in their packaging of the product. This is their strategy. And for all intents and purposes, most of us would love to believe that the companies that sell the most durable, the most effective and the least expensive products should be the ones worthy of our hard-earned bucks. This isn't the way capitalism works. Both companies had a budget, but only one company had a strategy. Amazingly enough, the one with the strategy has inferior products and services, nevertheless, they are the ones that will get more of our money. This is because they learned the value of strategic thinking.

When a disciple (follower or disciplined person) merges his or her creativity (wisdom) together, a leader is born. A leader is a forever student who also serves as a teacher; this means that a leader can never stop learning or growing. True leaders read books, have mentors and exercise their wisdom on a daily basis. True leaders run towards problems, not away from them. As a leader, you have to locate where you are on the Leaders' Spectrum, and you must monitor your own growth. Even more, you need someone to monitor your growth with you; this is why we need mentors or advisors.

Let's look at the Leaders' Spectrum again, but this time, I've listed some of the traits for each category.

Consumers/ Complainers	Spectators/ Procrastinators	Producers/ Solutionists/Doers
Complains about everything	Gossips because of immaturity, but will also silence other complainers from time to time	Has a solution or an idea for every problem presented
Liability to any organization	An asset and a liability	An asset to any organization

Consumers/ Complainers	Spectators/ Procrastinators	Producers/ Solutionists/Doers
Has problems	Sees problems but says nothing to leadership	Has solutions
A taker. Consumers are always in need; they take far more than they give.	Won't take much and won't give much. Most spectators are in a phase where they are too prideful and afraid to ask for help, therefore, they become self-reliant.	A giver. Solutions are full of ideas, for example, rather than saying the ink is low in the printer, producers will show up with a new ink cartridge or, in some cases, a whole new printer!
Prideful/ entitled/immature	Fearful/independent/immature, but hopefully, in the process of maturing.	Humble/grateful/mature
Cold	Lukewarm	Hot

Get this. Every company, organization and leader needs a healthy balance of imbalanced people. While they can be frustrating to deal with, they unknowingly help us to see the kinks in our armor; they help us to hear and see the problems that rise up in whatever it is that we're attempting to build or lead. However, an imbalanced structure will always topple over. This is why, as a leader, you have to take on the personal task of raising up other leaders; you have to be willing to invest time, energy and effort into duplicating yourself. Again, this doesn't mean that you need to raise up emulators; trust me, you want everyone to be comfortable in their own skin and in their own authenticity. Nevertheless, when I say you have to duplicate yourself, I'm speaking of your discipline. You have to identify every person following your lead as either a complainer/consumer, spectator/procrastinator or a producer/solutionist. This is called strategizing. What you're doing is identifying your key players so that you can put them in their rightful positions. This is why so many companies and organizations fail within the first few years. Investopedia reported the following, "It's often said that more than half of new businesses fail during the first year. According to the Small Business Association (SBA), this isn't necessarily true. The SBA states that only 30% of new businesses fail during the first two years of being open, 50% during the first five years and 66% during the first 10. The SBA goes on to state that only 25% make it to 15 years or more. Though the odds are better than the commonly held belief, there are still many businesses that are closing down every year in the United States" (Source: Investopedia/Top 6 Reasons New Businesses Fail/Michael T. Deane).

Again, every person on this spectrum is a leader. Complainers lead other complainers, spectators lead other spectators and producers teach and lead other producers. What's interesting is, we all start off as consumers/complainers. Think about an infant. Infants whine and complain about everything, but this doesn't mean that they are bad people or that they will remain immature for the duration of their lives. Some of them will remain immature because of poor leadership (parenting), while others will continue to move across the spectrum. As leaders outgrow the season of complaining, they will find themselves in a season of spectating. This is okay because we all need to have a few seasons of silence, meaning, there are times when we don't possess the wisdom, the skills or the tact needed to speak up. In other words, there's nothing wrong with being a spectator, just as long as you don't get stuck there. Most spectators eventually outgrow the season of spectating, and yet, they continue to do so because fear has paralyzed them. When this happens, they start leaning towards one or both sides of the spectrum. They will gossip about the problems they see, but when given the opportunity to speak up in a public arena, they will often relegate that responsibility to someone else. Or they will try to bypass the season of spectating prematurely; this is when you find people trying to usurp authority. Let me explain why this happens. None of these seasons have a timestamp on them. A consumer can end up remaining a consumer for decades on end. Why is this? This happens if and when the person refuses to sit still under a mentor long enough to be developed, pruned, tested and eventually sent out. Instead, the complainer leaves one church in search for another; they quit one job, hoping to find a company that will allow them to do as they please. They will even leave their marriages, looking for people they believe are better suited for them. All the same, most complainers don't have a regular study life; they always complain that they are too busy to read a book or show up at the meetings, the counseling sessions or the conferences. They prioritize their personal feelings over the big picture. Sadly enough, some people never stop complaining and some people never stop spectating, meaning, some people do stop growing. But thankfully, the same can be said about most producers. Some people never stop coming up with solutions. A great example of a mass producer is Thomas Edison. He has been credited with creating the practical light bulb, the motion picture camera, the phonograph, and more than a thousand other inventions. Thomas Edison has a total of 1,093 utility patents. Vincent Van Gogh created 2,100 artworks in just over a decade. Nelson Mandela was South Africa's first president. He led the anti-apartheid movement, helping South Africa to transition from apartheid to a multiracial democracy. He spent 27 years in prison for treason and sabotage; these charges would later be dropped.

Homework (Activation)

Locate yourself on the Leaders' Spectrum and write down five to ten bulletin points on what you plan to do to move into your rightful place (the producer's side).

The Jordan Effect

Michael Jordan is one of the most iconic sports figures in modern history. He retired from the NBA in 1999 and we still hear his name so often that one would think he's still in the league. There are a couple of lessons that we could learn from MJ to become valuable leadership creatives. The ultimate goal of leadership is influence. His name is so influential that nearly twenty years after his last game on the court, people still use his name in reference and comparison to the greats. He owns a large stake in the Charlotte Hornets, plus, he has stores, clothes and endorsements from Hanes, Gatorade and Upper Deck. He wasn't the best overall basketball player. *Don't stone me just yet.* He's had his share of troubles and failures; he's had his ups and his downs. However, if you say his name, just get ready for a great conversation. Let's not forget about his iconic shoe brand called Jordan's. People line up for days just to get a pair of these shoes. The shoes aren't made with a different kind of material than other shoes on the market. In fact, they keep releasing the same editions of the shoe on a consistent rotation. The shoes are a $3.1 billion dollar brand all within themselves. His shoes are so valuable that people have increased their homeowner's insurance policies just to cover the value of the shoes. Have you ever wondered what it is about the J's that causes people to stand in lines for days, go without paying their bills just to own them, or rob and even kill another human being just to own a pair? There is a critical leadership lesson here that we can learn from. I believe the lesson is the lesson of discipline. It is said that Michael Jordan practiced every day with the same intensity he had on the court. His philosophy was to practice harder than he played. Everyday, he devoted significant time to the fundamentals, not the dunks that would make the highlight reels of Sports Center. I think the world has robbed us of our love for fundamentals. I've noticed that every successful person seems to have a love affair with the basics.

I remember in High School when I got my first job. My goal was to save enough money to get a pair of Jordan's. I'll never forget that day I first put on a pair. The moment I put them on, something happened to me. I felt like I could fly like Mike. Instantly, I felt like a different person. I walked taller, I stood up longer, and I found reasons to be where people could see me because they had to see my shoes. I often wondered how those shoes managed to invigorate me, and I eventually discovered the secret. His discipline gave me confidence! But, here's the problem. When I took the shoes off, I no longer had that same vibe. Here is the critical lesson I learned from Jordan's—discipline is what builds confidence! That's a game-changer.

A lot of people leading nations, organizations, churches and businesses have reached their plateau because they lack discipline. Because of this, leadership is now a chore for them; it is no longer an experience or a privilege in their eyes. You will either become a leader who maintains an organization or grows it. "Everything rises and falls on leadership!" *Quote by John Maxwell.* Consistent, diligent self-investment is what grows the confidence and character needed for impactful leadership. It was Jordan's commitment to practice at five o'clock in the morning that made him great. He practiced free-throws; he didn't practice the dunks that made the highlight reels. Michael Jordan was the product of his thought-life. The same is true for Harriet Tubman. The journey towards success has nothing to do with building wealth; wealth is just a by-product of a sound thought-life. The journey towards success is all about finding peace, doing what you love to do and disciplining yourself. Leadership is helping others to do the same.

At this very moment, you are a product of your thought life. That should either make you jump for joy or want to throw this book away. *Don't do it!* You need a personal and honest assessment of where you are in life in order to progress. Had someone told me this earlier, I wouldn't have tried to "do leadership." Instead, I would have worked harder on my thought life to "produce leadership." I didn't evaluate my thoughts about myself, so I had to take what life gave me at face value. Most of us are guilty of this. We've allowed ourselves to become the sum total of our experiences, coupled with our reputations. This is an important concept to understand because we don't always do the hard work of introspection. It hurts, but it's necessary because it helps you to discover your "why." Impactful leadership is birthed from a strong sense of understanding your "why." The only way you can come to this place is to mull over the experiences that have impacted your life, take the wisdom from those experiences and use it to help others. You have to be willing to spend the rest of your life leading people up and out of the messes they made and into a disciplined life. You also have to be willing to change your mind over and over again; this is the process of maturation. It's sometimes a painful and uncomfortable process, but as we mature and learn to see the value of growing up, we learn to appreciate every growth spurt that we have. This is why reputations are oftentimes nothing but social constraints that keep us from evolving into the men and women that we have the potential to become. Over the course of our lives, we have been given nicknames; these nicknames had everything to do with our physical features, our shortcomings or the seasons we were in. For example, a man nicknamed "Shank" may have earned that nickname while he was in prison, and of course, his nickname would suggest that he used to create or use shanks. Once he's released from prison, he may carry that nickname with him, allowing it to become his street name. However, at some point, he may decide to give up the street life. His nickname was how he identified himself and how others identified him, so when he starts transitioning into a mature man, he would likely have to give up that nickname. Why? Because there is a reputation and an expectation attached to it. The nickname represented his former thought life, but his real name or new name represents his current thought life.

Your Belief System

Do you want to know why you think the way you do? You are the total sum of your beliefs, decisions, experiences and the perspectives formed from those experiences. When all of these components came together, they formed your "thought life." They formed the subconscious way in which you lead your life. I've found that the only way to get a grip on my decisions (which we will refer to from now on as "your do") was to get control of my identity (which we will refer to from now on as "your who"). What is an identity? It is how you see yourself and the report that you've accepted in relation to yourself. Your identity is what and who you identify with. I had to start challenging what I believed about myself. The vantage point by which you view yourself determines the quality of leadership decisions you'll make. If your identity has been negatively impacted by the decisions you made before you fully matured, and you are still identifying yourself by those choices, you are still in the middle of a wrestling match with your true identity.

I have to admit—I've seen great success in my life, however I think I've taken longer to reach this point than I should have because I didn't realize that I was my own curse. Let's be honest, we've all said that things would be better if we had more money, if we had better people around us or if someone would just help us achieve our goals. We tend to reason this way when we're transitioning between the old mindset and the new one. We tend to reason this way when we're on the wrong side of the spectrum. Once I stopped complaining, fantasizing and procrastinating, and once I did the hard work on my personal beliefs regarding myself, I finally started to gain traction in innovating my leadership. In other words, my thought life changed. What happened here was my belief system changed. Over the course of our lives, we've all experienced some drastic changes in our beliefs. There was a point when we believed in Santa Claus, the Easter Bunny, the Tooth Fairy and a host of fictional characters. This is because children don't guard their belief systems, and why should they, especially with their parents? Children normally believe everything that they're told. This is why they have to be protected, coached and disciplined. As we've grown older, we've experienced many changes to our belief systems. I think a large part of our growing up involves unbelieving some of the lies that we were told. Every belief serves as a foundation or a brick in what we call our belief system. If we stack a truth on top of a lie, the truth and the lie will go to war with one another. This is when we start asking a lot of questions; this is when we start making people promise to tell us the truth. And when a lie is discovered, we go through a mourning process because, as humans, we tend to give life to everything we believe. So, when something that we've accepted turns out to be a lie, we feel like we're pulling the plug on it. We have to watch it slip away right before our eyes. This is why, as leaders, we cannot be guilty of lying to people, even if what we are telling them, in our eyes, is nothing but a little white lie. Every lie sets the foundation for another lie, but every truth sets the foundation for more truth. Again, when these two come together, a war starts in our minds, and to restore our peace, we go on a mental pursuit looking for the truth.

Belief creates confidence. Confidence activates your leadership potential. People who truly believe in themselves are committed to manifesting their best selves. You have to be unwilling to accept the status quo, the labels, and the memories that were designed to imprison the leadership creative that's inside you. Do you believe that who you are today is a result of your experiences? I've found that most people no longer see themselves from a pure place. Life has happened to the best of us. Consequently, we've downplayed ourselves and renegotiated a lower value for ourselves. This is because the people that we know we have the potential to become seems to be so far under the rubbish of our experiences that we feel we're not worth the fight needed to unearth our identities. Did you know the most valuable substances are worth the dig? Lead yourself on an excavation mission to pull out your hidden treasure— leadership.

What are you confident in? Are you confident in yourself, your ideas, your leadership or your abilities? If you find insecurity in any arena of your thinking, please consider this —the belief system, again, is like a structure being built. There is line upon line and precept upon precept. When someone lays a brick down on a structure, they have to layer that brick with another brick. Every builder knows that it is unwise and even dangerous to throw wood in the mix with brick. So, they keep stacking the bricks until they are ready to create another foundation of sorts. A roof, believe it or not, is built on another foundation; we call this foundation the ceiling. The point is, if insecurity is in your life, this means that there is a brick or, better yet, a belief that you have, and you've been building on that belief for quite some time. Lies attract lies, meaning that whatever lie you started building on likely attracted more lies into your life. Maybe you were told that you weren't a good person or a good leader, and you built on this lie for several years. You've told yourself and others that you're not a great leader. This is a lie. Obviously, these beliefs go against everything else you believe, so it's created a level of instability in your life. We call this instability insecurity. So what has to happen is, those lies have to be located and removed, and you can't just stop there. You have to replace the lies with the truth. When this happens, insecurity will become a thing of the past because your belief system will become stable enough to endure every leadership challenge you face.

Self Discipline

Do you remember when you were in the first or second grade, and you didn't want to do your homework? You acted defeated to keep from completing the task, and in an effort to motivate you, either your parents or your teachers would say with enthusiasm, "You can do it ! You have to believe in yourself!" As elementary as it sounds saying this to adults, I have to remind you, "You have to believe in yourself!" I know that this is sometimes easier said than done because many people have never seen an example of a good leader; we've seen unstable people with titles and we've seen unstable people with authority, but we haven't seen many examples of healthy people who truly believe in their own leadership abilities. This is why one of the first steps that we have to take as leaders is through self-discipline. This helps us to create faith in our own abilities, which will, in turn, help us become confident leaders. This means that our disciplines aren't just physical, what we are doing is disciplining ourselves mentally and emotionally. What you believe about yourself will determine your value, your stamina and your direction as a leader.

I've heard it said, "If you think you can, you will; if you think you can't, you will." I personally know this to be true. Think better about yourself and your belief system will become healthy enough to produce a better leader. A better leader is a mentally and emotionally healthy leader. This is a leader who has become intentional about maturing and developing their skillsets; this is a leader who is intentional about overcoming the odds that are stacked against them. Remember, those odds are like faulty bricks; they have to be removed and replaced. You do this by replacing negative words with positive words. For example, if you've been called stupid your whole life, one of your disciplines involves overcoming this word and everything associated with it. You do this by removing this word from your vocabulary and replacing it with something positive. Some great replacement words would be "wise" or "intelligent." Dr. John Schafer wrote, "If the eyes are the window to the soul, then words are the gateway to the mind. Words represent thoughts. The closest one person can get to understanding another person's thoughts is to listen to the words that he or she speaks or writes. Certain words reflect the behavioral characteristics of the person who spoke or wrote them. I labeled these words, Word Clues. Word Clues increase the probability of predicting the behavioral characteristics of people by analyzing the words they choose when they speak or write" (Source: Psychology Today/Reading People by the Words They Speak). What you say about yourself is a reflection of what you think about yourself. What you say about others is a reflection of what you think about yourself. How you think about yourself will determine your effectiveness as a leader. What does this mean to us? Our discipline or lack thereof is directly tied to our belief systems. This is why we want to survey our hearts and remove every lie that we've been told, replace those lies with truths and continue to build our confidence and our self-discipline.

I believe the conversations and approaches to leadership need an upgrade. In my humble opinion, a person who just tells people what to do is not a leader. I know many people in leadership capacities. At this point, I've served as a leader for twenty years. My leadership opportunities started in my Uncle's church. At 15-years old, I started serving (apprenticing) under his leadership. I made myself available to be at his beck and call so that I could learn from him. I learned very quickly that in order to be a great leader, I had to first be a great apprentice. This is an important concept because it crafts your identity. Your ability to be the best at anything has to start in your willingness to dedicate yourself to someone or something greater than yourself. If you have to be forced into leadership, the character of a leader won't be produced. You must be willing and humble enough to receive instruction; this ensures that your foundation can stand the tests of time. I know plenty of people who have strong personalities, and these people have been labeled as leaders because their personalities are loud, but their persons are underdeveloped. Serving not only teaches you what to do, but it is used as a tool to constantly refine you and make you better. Being loud doesn't make you a leader, just like speeding towards a stop sign doesn't give you the right of way. Whoever arrived at that four-way stop first is the person who gets to release their breaks first, not the person who is clearly in a rush to get somewhere. Being a loud and aggressive leader normally means that you are wrestling with fear; it can also mean that, at some point in your life, someone dominated and controlled you. This person set the tone for your leadership, and now, you need to see an example of an emotionally stable leader so that you can pattern yourself after that leader, and not the one who abused and controlled you. This is why we have to be healed and we have to learn the art of self-discipline.

The Benefits of Discipline
I remember a time when I had served faithfully in the church for a solid five years. At that time, there was a process to ordination. You had to read and memorize a book we called the "Discipline." This manual had all of the church's doctrine, rules, policies and procedures inside it. If you could prove

that you had a genuine call from God and if you could answer spontaneous questions about the Discipline, the Bishop would ordain you—if he felt led to do so.

One day, I came to the church to do some work. I saw my Bishop there and asked him if I could purchase the book. The General Conference was coming up and I felt like I was ready to be ordained. He emphatically said NO. I was devastated. I felt like I was ready to be ordained; I believed that I deserved to be ordained. Why? It's simple— I felt like I was ready. At that time, I lived in Alton, Illinois and the church was in downtown St. Louis. For me, it was literally a three-hour trip to get to the church. At 16-years old, once my chores were completed, I would go to Alton Square Mall, get on the bus down to Granite City. From there, I would transfer to another bus and head down to East St. Louis. After this, I would get another transfer to the Metrolink train and take it over to the bus station at 8th and Pine. I'd wait for the West Florissant bus for twenty minutes, and then take it to the corner of West Florissant and Angelica. After all this, I would arrive at the church. I would do this every Tuesday, Wednesday and Friday. Not to mention, sometimes the service would be canceled (the church didn't have massive communication technology then). I would have to use the transfer from the W. Florissant bus to get on the Lee/Riveroads bus out to North County. This took another thirty minutes. I would then walk to my pastor's house to wait for my father or uncle to drive me back across the bridge to Alton. On Fridays, I would stay at my pastor's house for the entire weekend, and then go back to Alton Sunday night after church. I spent countless hours at the church helping in every department. I served him as his personal assistant, choir president (no, I can't sing), opened the church for prayer at five o'clock in the morning on Sunday mornings, plus, I physically cleaned the church for Friday night and Sunday morning services. I didn't mention that this building was a 450+ seater building, with a school building attached in the inner city of St. Louis.

When I turned 17-years old, my father felt that I should go into the military, but I felt led by God to stay in St. Louis to help my uncle with the church. Long story short, my father kicked me out of the house and I had to live with my uncle until I was 21-years old. I felt I couldn't repay him for his kindness to me, so I was determined to help him in any way. His NO was a test of my pride. Did I want to leave? Yep! I learned that leaving wouldn't hurt him, it would have hurt me. How I handled his NO was God qualifying if my YES was legitimate. (Note: Don't buy the lie that because you're gifted, you don't need a mentor. Even the greatest athletes have coaches. Realize that your leader's imperfections are a gift to your development. Be a learner, not a runner!) People who run never reap the benefits of stability. They spend their lives being controlled by their emotions, running from one church to another and serving one pastor after another. I served my pastor for another five years before he decided to ordain me. I never left him. I've been in the ministry now for twenty-plus years and I am still learning from him. Do I regret sticking by him? No! This has helped to develop me as a leader; it birthed patience and endurance in me, both of which are the foundations of self-discipline.

Managing Your Thought Life

There are three types of people in this world, and both groups are either bound or liberated by their mindsets. There are problem-solvers (producers), spectators (procrastinators) and problem-creators (consumers). First off, we are all creators; let's establish this truth before we move forward. We are naturally and instinctively creative. But what we create determines the direction of our leadership. A problem-solver creates solutions to problems; this is why they are called solutionists. A problem-creator creates problems and then complains about them. Think of a child. A child will eat all of the food in a house, and then complain about being hungry. This is because children are naturally immature, therefore, they create problems. Why are children immature? Because they lack information! Information is the key to maturity. A parent, on the other hand, should be mature. The parent sees the problem of the empty refrigerator and solves the problem by working to earn a paycheck; this way, the parent can restock the refrigerator as it's being emptied out. As the child matures, he learns to feed himself. If the refrigerator is empty, a maturing child will point out the fact that it's empty, but won't place too much emphasis on the empty refrigerator. Instead, children are known to ask others for money or they'll ask to spend the night at a friend or relative's house when there is no food in their own homes; this is innovative thinking that shows that the child is in the process of maturing. What is the child doing? It's called seeking peace. Hungry people are not at peace; this is why their stomachs growl. When we're hungry, we seek peace by trying to find something to eat. When we're thirsty, we seek peace by trying to find something to drink. When we're in pain, we seek peace by looking for pain-killers. When our bladders are full, we seek peace by going to a bathroom. Michael Jordan had a problem that needed solving. His problem was that he was gifted and he needed somewhere to express that gift. I'm sure that when he saw people playing basketball, he would become agitated and shout at the television. This is because his gift could no longer be silent. Now, this problem could have manifested itself in many ways. Gifted people don't always use their gifts for good; some gifted folks use their gifts for evil. For example, a lot of drug dealers are gifted to do business, but perversion took over their thought-life, and now, they use their gifts to do evil.

Again, the journey towards success is all about finding peace and helping others to do the same. You do this by successfully changing the way that you think. If you are going to become an impactful leader, the first person that you have to impact is yourself. The first person you have to lead is yourself. You don't do this by networking and creating a snazzy website. You do this by reading books, going to conferences, getting yourself a mentor, watching videos and presenting yourself in environments where sound information is constantly being released. In other words, you have to see yourself as a sponge. Whatever atmospheres you place yourself in are the atmospheres that you will eventually begin to set.

How do you manage your thought-life? Below, are a few pointers.

- **Specialized knowledge is power.** General information is beneficial, but specialized knowledge allows you to focus in a specific area that eventually makes you an authority. For example, let's say that you are a beautician and you "do hair." The power is in "the type of hair" you have knowledge in, not just the general knowledge of hair.
- **Understanding is key.** If knowledge is the door to success, then understanding is the key. For example, you can know or memorize all of the traffic signs on a highway, but if you don't understand what they mean, you will put yourself and others in grave danger every time you crank up a car.
- **Wisdom is the principal thing.** If knowledge is a door and understanding is the key to that door, this could only mean that wisdom is the wealth behind the door. Wisdom is understanding with interest attached to it. This means that you get the knowledge, get the understanding and you allow the two to marinate until they become wisdom.
- **Get healed.** A lot of people hear about the value of a sound mind, but they don't understand why it's so important for them to get healed. So, they become ambitious and anxious; they rush to be on platforms

because they think that they can drown out the sound of their pain if they turn the mic up loud enough. Hurt people hurt people; they've heard this adage, but again, because they lack understanding, it is nothing more than a cute quote to them. Because of this, they rush towards the limelight, hurting themselves all the more along the way. By the time they get the attention they want, their hearts' wounds are seeping with bitterness. They then begin to hurt others in their attempts to redeem themselves. Before you do anything, go see a therapist. A mentally healthy leader is a valuable leader.

- **Get involved.** A lot of people underestimate the power of community and charity. You were designed to be a giver, not just to yourself, but to others. LiveScience reported the following, "People who volunteer for selfless reasons, such as helping others, live longer than those who don't lend a helping hand, a new study shows. However, those who volunteer for more self-centered reasons do not reap the same life-extending benefits" (Source: Live Science/People Who Volunteer Live Longer, Study Suggests/Remy Melina). Put your hands to the plow and help to dig others out of their ditches. The more you dig to help others, the more you'll learn and the more you'll uncover and have confidence in your leadership potential.
- **Get a vision.** You have to have a destination in mind. Create a vision board and map out your five-year

plan, your ten-year plan and your twenty-year plan. Also create an overall life plan. This gives you an idea of where you're going and the motivation you'll need to get there.

Remember, your thought-life is stabilized or destabilized by what you believe regarding yourself. This is why unstable leaders have unstable followers. Examine your heart daily, and if you find insecurity anywhere in your life, address it and replace it with the truth. If you do this enough, your confidence will be restored and your thought-life will become a healthy, productive and happy one!

Homework (Activation)

1. Make a list of your insecurities.
2. Trace every insecurity that you have, for example, one insecurity that I had was about my eyes. This insecurity could be traced back to my childhood when children would tease me about the size of my eyes. Your insecurity may be about the way you speak, your walk, your nose, your skin color, your leadership, etc. Trace all of your insecurities; find the root of them all.
3. Once you've traced all your insecurities, reject the lies that you were told and replace those lies with truths. For example, if you were told that you aren't that smart, renounce that lie and then, write down, I am intelligent!

You Have Big Eyes (Vision)

We all have something about us that makes us insecure. When I was a kid, I found myself always being teased about how big my eyes were. This bred insecurity in me, so I would try to hide my eyes by wearing glasses, even though I didn't need them. Whenever I look at old pictures of myself, I laugh at the length I went to cover up my eyes. The glasses would be too small and you could see how tight they were because of the marks they left on the side of my face.

I eventually begin to see a correlation between my attempt to hide my eyes with the dimming of my vision; this is because I have always been a big dreamer. Oftentimes, small-minded people will make fun of you because they want you to downsize your vision. As leaders, we often do this to ourselves as well; we do this by downplaying our strengths and highlighting our weaknesses. This is so small-minded people will feel better about themselves. I eventually realized that my big eyes were a reflection of my big vision to change the world. I want to use my life to make a difference. Leadership, to me, is about creating a great vision—one that makes the world a better place and enlightens people, helping them to realize their greatness and their potential to become the change this world needs to see. What's your vision? Has life, circumstances, people or insecurity made you hide and collapse your vision? Vision is the ability to take a concept from your imagination and bring it into reality. It's a part of our ability as humans to be creators. Where there is nothing, making something. See problems as possibilities, make your potential potent and make what's abstract a reality.

Most people would describe vision as the ability to see (verb) or the state of having sight (noun). And while these definitions are true, they are limited. The true definition of vision is having the courage to see. Why courage? Because, as humans, we intentionally focus on the things and the people that appear to be well put together; we look away whenever we see problems, whether those problems are world hunger, the cancer epidemic or racism. We do this because we don't like seeing problems that we have the inability or the courage to confront or fix. We often parallel vision with blindness, but what exactly is blindness? If you said the inability to see, you are absolutely correct, but why can't the person see? What has constricted or limited the individual's vision? The point is, blindness is not always the state of the physical person, it can also reflect the conditions or environment the person is in. For example, if I took you to a warehouse where there were no windows and turned off all of the lights, you'd be blind in that moment. But you are not physically blind, there is something prohibiting you from seeing and that, of course, is darkness.

Darkness, in the corporate world, is symbolic of ignorance.

Ignorance is a disease of the mind, but the issue with ignorance is, there is a cure for it. It's called information. You can get information from a book and/or a mentor. This means that ignorance is a curable disease; it is a willful act. Children are the exception, of course. Children who are limited to only the information fed to them by their parents, their communities and their schools are ignorant, but not by choice. Once they become adults, most of them graduate to being willfully ignorant. This is why we need leaders like you to get the discipline, the information and the tools needed to start your journey towards the producers' side of the spectrum. You are needed! This is also why you can't keep procrastinating and making excuses. If you have a book idea, write and finish it. If you want to launch a business, do it! But to do any of this, you have to have a vision. You also have to measure the cost of the vision and be patient enough to see it through.

I want you to imagine this. A man sees a vision of a huge farm. It's beautifully manicured, spacious and full of life. He imagines turning the farm into a zoo of sorts, allowing people to tour the farm Monday through Saturday for a small fee. Excited, he starts looking for a property to start his farm on. He plans to live in the main house, but he wants also to create a small, high-end hotel on the property as well. He also wants a spa and a gym on the property. And finally, he plans to create an area for kids where they will be able to ride donkeys, go into the park or play in the pool. Excited, he goes on the hunt, looking for the land he'll need to get the ball rolling on his idea. He eventually finds the perfect property and buys it. He starts pricing everything else he'll need to make his dream come to pass, only to find that he can't even afford the farm animals. Looking at his net pay, he determines that, in order for the full vision to be manifested, he will need to save a large portion of his pay for the next 12 years. What would you do in a situation like this? Most people would give up on their dreams. They'd sell the property and continue working a job that they hated until they're old enough to retire from it. You have to know that every vision has a price tag attached to it, and while that price tag may be steep, if it is your dream, it is well worth the price. It's up to you, however, to determine if the end-result is worth the time, effort and tears. Most people decide that it's not worth it. They don't express this out loud, but they express it by not starting the business, writing the book, launching the organization or fighting for their families.

Again, it's great to have a big vision. As a matter of fact, show me a man with a small vision and I'll show you a man who's allowing fear and/or the opinions of people to constrict the size of his vision! With big vision comes a hefty-sized price tag. The currency that you have to invest may not be in the form of dollars and cents. Your currency may be your time, your blood, your sweat and your tears. Some visions even cost you a few relationships, but again, you have to personally determine if the vision is worth the sacrifices attached to it. People who make the necessary sacrifices to see their visions come to pass rarely regret making those sacrifices. So, if you're the guy who needs 12 years to see his vision come to pass, my advice to you would be:

1. **Wait!** Be patient and make it a point to continue adding to your vision. This helps to keep you interested in it.
2. **Learn!** Utilize this time to learn as much as you can about whatever it is that you want to build, whether it be a business or a family.
3. **Plan!** Benjamin Franklin went on record saying, "If you fail to plan, you are planning to fail!" Create a blueprint. Ask around. Get your contracts together. Whatever you do, don't forget to plan!
4. **Sacrifice!** People who are not willing to sacrifice anything to watch their visions come to pass end up sacrificing their visions and accepting anything that is thrown their way. One of the most rejected keys to success is sacrifice.
5. **Conquer!** Nike said it this way, "Just do it!"

Because I have big vision, I've always been fascinated by people who've launched great careers, companies or organizations. For example, most of us are familiar with Sam Walton. He is the founder of Walmart. Here's a snippet of his timeline:

- **1940:** He started working at a local J.C. Penny store. While working there, his boss threatened to fire him, saying that he was not cut out for retail.
- **1942:** He was drafted into the United States Army. He served stateside as a communications officer in the

Army Intelligence Corps during World War II.

- **1943:** He married the love of his life, Helen Robson Walton.
- **1945:** He was honorably discharged from the military. He also took $5,000 of his own money and $20,000 that he'd borrowed from his father-in-law and launched a Ben Franklin variety store in Newport, Arkansas. He tripled his business, and by 1950, he owned the leading Ben Franklin store within his region.
- **1950:** His landlord refused to renew Mr. Walton's lease because he refused to sell the store to the landlord. The landlord wanted to purchase the company for his son.
- **1950:** He opened Walton's Five & Dime. He found immeasurable success with this venture as well.
- **1962:** After being denied a loan to launch his new idea for a discount store (Walmart), Mr. Walton decided to mortgage his home. After this, he opened his first Walmart store in Rogers, Arkansas. By 1969, he owned 18 Walmart stores throughout Arkansas and Missouri.
- **1980:** Sam Walton had 276 stores, with an opening rate of more than 100 new stores each year.
- **1985:** Forbes Magazine reported that Mr. Walton was the richest man in America, with a worth of $2.8 billion.

Walmart's current net worth (not gross) is $324 billion. And what amazes me the most is that Sam Walton's journey was not without opposition. His landlord had refused to renew his lease simply because he'd refused to sell his company to him. The same year that Walmart was launched, other competitors like Kmart and Woolco came on the scene. Sam Walton died of bone cancer in 1992.

Visionaries come in all sizes, shapes, colors and genders. Another great visionary whose life is worth examining is Oprah Winfrey. Let's look at her timeline:

- **1954:** Oprah was born into poverty in Kosciusko, Mississippi.
- **1963:** Oprah was raped at the age of 9. Sexual abuse became a theme of her childhood.
- **1968:** Oprah became pregnant at the age of 14. Her son died shortly after being born.
- **1971:** She won the Miss Black Tennessee pageant.
- **1978:** She became both the youngest news anchor and the first black female news anchor with WJZ-TV, where she co-hosted the show, People Are Talking, alongside Richard Sher.
- **1984:** Oprah relocated to Chicago to co-host AM Chicago, which was WLS-TV's low-rated half-hour morning talk-show.
- **1985:** Oprah was cast as Ms. Sophia, a strong, mouthy and loving woman who refused to bow down to the oppression that Black women faced in the South during the early 1900s.
- **1986:** The Oprah Winfrey Show begins.

We all know the iconic Oprah Winfrey. Today, her net worth is an astonishing $2.8 billion. And of course, leadership is not always about what you can personally earn from your disciplines. We've had leaders like Rosa Parks, Dr. Myles Munroe and many others who've pioneered different movements. They all had a vision; they all had a dream, but unlike most people, they didn't allow their dreams to stay locked away in their fantasies. Instead, they decided to push through all of the opposition and make their dreams a reality.

"I have a dream!" Martin Luther King, Jr.'s speech was one of the most prolific speeches that we've ever heard. He detailed his vision to the masses—a vision of equality and peace between races. Of course, there were people on both sides of the Black/White spectrum who did not share his vision. Some Whites fancied themselves as being non-prejudiced; they fought for civil rights, but they wanted racial segregation to remain intact. This means that they were both racist and compassionate. This may sound far-fetched, but there are people out there who hate to see others oppressed, but at the same time, they don't want the oppressed to live in their communities. Some Whites wanted things to stay as they were or to return to how they had once been. They saw African Americans as nothing but second-class citizens who needed to be controlled, monitored and kept in bondage. The same is true for some African-Americans. Some Blacks were prejudiced themselves because of all the injustices they'd fallen victim to. They wanted to be separate, but equal. Malcolm X was an example of someone who supported this theory. Both Malcolm X. and Martin Luther King were men who had visions that they believed would empower the Black race. Both of their visions were backed by their religious beliefs, of course. But Dr. King's vision received more momentum because it was all about love as a whole. He didn't see the need for us to separate ourselves from one another. He simply wanted reconciliation between both races; he wanted us to learn to love one another and embrace our differences. As a part of his infamous speech, Martin Luther King, Jr. said:

> *"I say to you today, my friends, so even though we face the difficulties of today and tomorrow, I still have a dream. It is a dream deeply rooted in the American dream.*
>
> *I have a dream that one day this nation will rise up and live out the true meaning of its creed: 'We hold these truths to be self-evident: that all men are created equal.'*
>
> *I have a dream that one day on the red hills of Georgia the sons of former slaves and the sons of former slave owners will be able to sit down together at the table of brotherhood.*
>
> *I have a dream that one day even the state of Mississippi, a state sweltering with the heat of injustice, sweltering with the heat of oppression, will be transformed into an oasis of freedom and justice.*
>
> *I have a dream that my four little children will one day live in a nation where they will not be judged by the color of their skin but by the content of their character.*

I have a dream today.
I have a dream that one day, down in Alabama, with
its vicious racists, with its governor having his lips
dripping with the words of interposition and
nullification; one day right there in Alabama, little
black boys and black girls will be able to join hands
with little white boys and white girls as sisters and
brothers.
I have a dream today.
I have a dream that one day every valley shall be
exalted, every hill and mountain shall be made low,
the rough places will be made plain, and the crooked
places will be made straight, and the glory of the Lord
shall be revealed, and all flesh shall see it together."

Dr. King was mapping out his vision for the world to embrace. But his dream was of the future; it is a dream that we're still waiting to see come fully to pass. This is because Mr. King was casting vision; he was detailing a dream that he had, and we all know that he worked tirelessly and selflessly to see this dream come to pass before his life was tragically cut short. He was assassinated on April 4th, 1968. Six years later, his mother would be shot by a Black man with extremist views. Alberta King was killed on June 30th,1974 at Ebenezer Baptist Church. Wikipedia details the story this way; it reads, "Alberta King was shot and killed on June 30, 1974, at age 69, by Marcus Wayne Chenault, a 23-year-old black man from Ohio who had adopted an extremist version of the theology of the Black Hebrew Israelites.

Chenault's mentor, Rev. Hananiah E. Israel of Cincinnati, castigated black civil rights activists and black church leaders as being evil and deceptive, but claimed in interviews not to have advocated violence. Chenault did not draw any such distinction, and actually first decided to assassinate Rev. Jesse Jackson in Chicago, but canceled the plan at the last minute. Two weeks later he set out for Atlanta, where he shot Alberta King with two handguns as she sat at the organ of the Ebenezer Baptist Church. Chenault said that he shot King because 'all Christians are my enemies,' and claimed that he had decided that black ministers were a menace to black people. He said his original target had been Martin Luther King, Sr., but he had decided to shoot his wife instead because she was near him. He also killed one of the church's deacons, Edward Boykin, in the attack, and wounded another woman."

Marcus Wayne Chenault was another example of the blind being led by the blind. He died in prison at the age of 44 from a stroke. This is why we need visionaries, not just leaders with vision, but leaders with good visions.

This is the price of vision. Martin Luther King, Jr. knew the cost of his vision. He went on record saying, "We've got some difficult days ahead, but it really doesn't matter to me now, because I've been to the mountain top, and I don't mind. Like anybody, I would like to live a long life—longevity has its place. But I'm not concerned about that now. I just want to do God's will. And He's allowed me to go up to the mountain. And I've looked over and I've seen the Promised Land. I may not get there with you, but I want you to know tonight that we, as a people, will get to the Promised Land. And so I'm happy tonight; I'm not worried about anything; I'm not fearing any man. Mine eyes have seen the glory of the coming of the Lord." He said, "I may not get there with you." This was Dr. King's way of acknowledging the price he would pay for coming against the stronghold of racism.

I don't know what you're building. Maybe, it's a church; maybe, it's a family or maybe, it's a business. Like me, you have big eyes (vision), but have you counted the cost associated with the vision? Rosa Parks was escorted off a bus in handcuffs because she was sitting around small-minded people. Martin Luther King, Jr. paid the ultimate price for his vision. Prince Harry, along with his wife, Meghan Markle recently took a step back from their royal duties. This news came as a shock to everyone in the UK, including the queen herself. But get this, having a vision sometimes means that you have to step back and renounce everyone else's plans for you so that you can dream without interference.

I have big eyes, and one day, I got tired of hiding them. I took off my sunglasses and started showing off my eyes. Eventually, I realized my big eyes weren't a deformity, they were and are one of my most prized features. I stopped minimizing who I am to accommodate the opinions of small-minded people. I soon realized that my desire to change and impact the world was directly tied to my vision.

Homework (Activation)

Write your full vision out on paper or type it in a word document. Don't stop writing until you are intimidated by your vision. Next, write three bullet points under each major event that you see, detailing how you plan to carry out that event. For example:

Write a book

1. Give myself the deadline of September 14th of this year to finish!
2. Take a writers' course starting next month.
3. Start paying on my publishing package now.

Start a spa

1. Finish my degree and get my cosmetology license by the end of this year.
2. Get my business license by April of next year.
3. Create a list of some of the products and services I want to sell, and I'll do this on today!

Get in shape

1. Limit my sugar intake by 90 percent.
2. Get a gym membership and go, at minimum, three days a week for one hour each visit.
3. Cut carbs out of my diet by at least 98 percent.

Maturing as a Leader

What is a leader? We all have a standardized idea of what a leader is and what a leader does, but the majority of us don't understand the nature or overall responsibility of a leader. It is for this reason that so many people get into leadership roles and abuse their positions. Most of us have had to serve under egotistical, self-serving and abusive leaders. We've had to work in stressful atmospheres and we've had to pray while driving to work just to get through another day. And the sad part is, many of us have only seen poor examples of leadership, so whenever we took our first leadership roles, we were just as abusive as our predecessors. This is because our former (or current) leaders created a mold or a profile, and we thought that being a leader meant that we had to deform our character until it could fit into that mold. In other words, we forsook our own identities and buried our personalities for the sole purpose of "fitting into someone else's shoes." And it is also for this reason that the world is filled with rebels. Rebels are people who have decided to take leadership roles, but their leadership is in direct opposition to someone else's leadership. This is also why good leaders have to oftentimes lead rebellious people. Many people today are hurt; they are terrified of submission and they hate anyone who stands in a position of authority. This is because, once again, some people have never seen a healthy example of a leader. They were abused by their parents, neglected by their own families, betrayed by their friends and groomed by the people who were preying on them.

Every leader has to grow through several stages. They include:
- Unrealistic expectations
- Misrepresentations of their character
- Procrastination
- True representation

How we respond to each stage is a showmanship of our maturity level. And get this; it's perfectly okay to be immature. We have all been immature at some point in our lives, and we are all still immature in some areas of our lives, so don't be in a rush to mature. As the old folks used to say, "Don't be in a rush to grow up!" I believe that most of us wish we'd listened to them back then because the responsibilities and expectations associated with every stage of our lives continue to mount as we grow older or mature. The more mature you are, the more you're going to be pulled on, stretched and misunderstood. Immature people don't understand the language of mature people. That's like expecting a two-year old to understand the stock market. As leaders, we all develop at our own paces and we all struggle with certain issues as we develop.

Unrealistic Expectations

A leader's profile isn't a stone sculpture of his or her face, of course, but for the sake of this presentation, I want you to imagine a mold of your face being made. Now, I want you to mentally take this mold and ask the people who are following you to put their faces in it. What you will discover is that none of their faces would fit into this mold. Some people's faces would be too big, some people's faces would be too small, and some people's faces would be the right size, but their features would be too small or too prominent. What this means is that you are the only version of yourself on the face of this Earth; you are the only version of yourself to ever live. Nevertheless, you are creating a mold, but not a mold of your face, but a mold of your character. We use the concept of "fitting into someone else's shoes," when what we're really saying is that we're fashioning another human being as a mold or an example for us to pattern ourselves after. Following in someone's footsteps is not the greatest concept that we've come up with. This gives people the false idea that their lives should mirror the lives of others. Do you know that there are young men who've committed suicide because they believed that they were supposed to emulate their fathers? Their fathers had been powerful, and sometimes even wealthy men, and our society describes them as "having big shoes to fill." This is exactly what the world did to Bobbi Kristina Brown—Whitney Houston and Bobby Brown's daughter. People expected her to sound like her mother, and as beautiful and as talented as she was within her own right, she didn't have the same level of gifting that her mother had. Howbeit, because she was young and underdeveloped, she kept trying to silence her naysayers. Bobbi Kristina Brown died on July 26th, 2015, and it was after her death that we saw a lot of people starting to speak positively about her. She died doing what young people are known to do—she messed around with drugs, plus, she was surrounded by parasitic people.

This young lady had been pressured by an unforgiving society to become who she was not. And while we can't for sure say that this is what drove her to drugs or into the arms of Nick Gordon, the man who would eventually be found legally, but not criminally, responsible for Ms. Brown's death, we can say that she had to deal with the pressures of fame, the sudden trauma of her mother's death and a society that does not always reward good. As a leader, this is why you absolutely have to mature. When the topic of maturing in leadership is brought up in any conversation with emerging leaders, you will always notice an awkward silence in the room. This is because many millennial leaders-to-be are more focused on platforms than they are on maturing. As your character is being developed, there are going to be people out there who will constantly remind you that you are nothing like your predecessors; they want you to believe that you are inferior to them or you should just take a seat in mediocrity. This is why maturation isn't just a cute word that got dropped into the leadership conversations, maturation is a necessity for any and every leader! When you're immature, the words from these people can be emotionally, mentally and spiritually devastating. A lot of people are wounded or dead today because they came out too soon; they tried to show off their leadership too soon. Think of a baby's brain. When a newborn first enters the Earth, the baby's skull has what we call soft spots. These soft spots give the baby's head the flexibility it needs to go through its mother's womb. It also allows the baby's brain and skull to grow and develop. When a baby has soft spots, we are careful with how we carry the baby. We won't allow other kids to play with the infant because they could unintentionally harm the baby. Now, think of a mold. When it's first created, it is soft because it's made of clay. It has to harden before it's displayed to the public. If it's displayed prematurely, it could easily be conformed, damaged or broken. For example, imagine a wet mold on display at a museum. Some woman comes along and places her hand on the wet mold. Consequently, the mold ends up hardening with her fingerprints on it. These fingerprints represent trauma. Every leader goes through stages; there are stages of immaturity, stages of procrastination, and finally, there is maturity. Maturity, of course, is not a stage; it's more like when the skull hardens. This is when the leader has taken his or her position, and the leader has become fully developed.

Bobbi Kristina, while not a prominent figure, is a perfect example of an underdeveloped leader. She needed someone more mature than herself, someone who had her best interest at heart to cover and lead her. This was the empty seat in her life, and unfortunately, she decided to allow Nick Gordon to fill that seat. She was no Whitney

Houston, but I'm confident that if she had been placed under the right tutors and if she was still alive today, she would be or would eventually have become a superstar. She had talents and gifts, but she didn't exactly understand her full potential. She was still in the youth of her development; she was still trying to fit her mother's shoes to pacify a bunch of naysayers. This is why every leader needs a leader, and not just any leader, but someone who has been where they are trying to go. Every leader needs someone to tell them when they need more development, where they need more development and how to get the development they need. Every leader needs someone who has the power to sit them down when they are immature and to raise them up when they are ready to go before the world. An underdeveloped leader will always compare himself or herself to other leaders. An underdeveloped leader will spend more time addressing his or her naysayers than the leader does developing his or her gifts. You can always tell when a leader is immature because they'll typically create silly posts or share foolish memes, for example, underdeveloped leaders will spend an excessive amount of time addressing their haters. Every other post they share is about themselves or their haters. This means that the leader is too distracted to lead; the leader is too immature to platform his or her gift. What does an underdeveloped leader need? The answer is clear—they need more development. An underdeveloped leader needs more information.

I want you to imagine a potter sitting at a wheel, but in the middle of that wheel, I don't want you to imagine a lump of wet clay. I want you to imagine your brain. Your brain, of course, represents your mindset. I want you to imagine that, starting off, your brain was the size of a pea and the shape of a square. The potter starts the wheel and begins to add more clay to your mindset. This clay represents information. Every leader needs an overabundance of information if he or she is going to be an effective or impactful leader. Leaders who lack information are people who are full of opinions; these people are controlled by their emotions, meaning, they are immature. Imagine the wheel turning and the clay or information being added. As the potter adds new information to your brain, he puts his hands on your mind and begins to put pressure on it so that you can stop being square; he puts pressure on it to give it the shape that he wants. But you can feel this pressure. When the knowledge was added to you, you were happy, but when that knowledge started being pressed into your mind, it disrupted your normal pattern of thinking. So, how did you respond? When you were immature, more than likely, you responded by complaining, by quitting and by crying. Over the years, you've matured, so you've learned to respond in a different way. You came to realize that the pressure, albeit uncomfortable, was necessary for you to become the impactful leader that you are today or the impactful leader that you will become in the near future. We all love learning something new, but it's almost as if information has to be massaged into our heads, otherwise, it'll be nothing more than just untested knowledge. Our experiences in life help us to take this information and give life to it. So, for example, if someone told me that in order to sustain a healthy marriage, a man would need to know when to lead and when to be humble enough to receive instructions from his wife, that information would be helpful, just not timely. This is invaluable knowledge, but because I'm unmarried, it doesn't do much for me. When I do get married, however, I would have to take this knowledge from my mental savings account and start using it. Before marriage, this information would be nice to have, but useless to me; that is, unless I was sharing it with a couple that I was counseling. But the minute I need to apply this information to my own life is the moment that it takes on a life of its own. This is when the information becomes invaluable to me. What I'm saying is, as a leader, you have to always submit your mind to new information; yes, even information that doesn't necessarily seem relevant to you today.

Misrepresentation

There is a famous biblical character that most of us are familiar with. His name is Moses. He was born in Egypt, and his parents, like the rest of the Jews in Egypt at that time, were in bondage. Pharaoh was terrified of their potential, so he increased their workload and their oppression. Eventually, Pharaoh commanded that all of the male children should be killed immediately upon exiting their mother's wombs. The midwives didn't follow Pharaoh's instructions, and Moses was born. Moses' mother hid him for three months, and when she realized that she could no longer hide him, she put him in a basket and placed the basket on the edge of the river. Pharaoh's daughter found Moses and decided to raise him as her own. The short of the story is, God used Moses to set His people free from Egyptian bondage. This amazing story is filled with miracles, signs, wonders, catastrophes and victories. Moses is definitely a man that we should all want to pattern ourselves after. He was a true leader, an overcomer and a deliverer. But that's not the point I want to make. I want to talk about a famous sculpture created by the famous and prized painter, Michelangelo himself, that falsely depicts the face of Moses. He created a sculpture of the famed patriarch, and this would be great if he had not added horns to the sculpture. Why did he do this? He misinterpreted the Bible. You see, Moses had received the Ten Commandments while meeting with God on Mount Sinai. According to the scriptures, when he'd come off the mountain, his countenance was so glorious that the Israelites could not look directly at him. Some translations of the Bible said that his face "shone." This word could be interpreted as "radiance" or "horns." Michelangelo obviously chose the latter.

Why did I share this story with you? The sculpture was not a rendition of Moses' character, but of his physical body. It was a gross misrepresentation of his character, even if it was produced as the result of ignorance. Any person who had never read about Moses would be curious to know who he was if that person had come face to face with this famous sculpture. If they simply saw the sculpture, they would be led to assume that Moses was an evil and maybe even a devilish man. I say that to say that people are going to memorialize you (yes, even while you are alive), and they will create molds and profiles of you that do not truly depict your character. This means that, as a leader, you have to be willing to be misunderstood. A leader who is passionate about making sure that everyone understands him or her is a leader who's too distracted to lead. Leadership is about you modeling the mentality that you want others to wear, and being fully unbothered by the people who misrepresent you.

No one is immune from misrepresentation, including the human race as a whole. Evolutionists believe that humans were once monkeys; they believe that time has not only reshaped our ways of reasoning, but time has reshaped our physical features, our posture and our mindsets. Of course, this is not true, but as humans, we have developed more because of technological advances, not in our features, but in our minds. This means that we are advancing towards something; we are mentally and spiritually evolving, but what are we becoming? The term "evolution" suggests that we are becoming something, but what? This means that the theory of evolution is nothing but man's attempt to explain what he couldn't possibly understand. I want you to imagine the facial profile of what archaeologists and evolutionists believe to be the features of a caveman. Imagine a side-view of his face. Chances are, you're imaging a man who looks remarkably like an ape. A caveman wasn't that smart; he was more like the cross between a man and an animal. Now, if evolutionists were right in their assessments, the story of

Adam and Eve would be a complete fabrication, which would discredit the entire Bible. This would also mean that mankind has been developing for millions of years, but what we have been developing into is a complete mystery. Again, this is unfounded because even nature tells us that everything that lives and breathes in the Earth is a reproduction of something; everything that grows is growing into something. What you pattern yourself after or who you pattern yourself after is the very thing or the very person that is serving as a leader or a template in your life. This is the very essence of leadership. Leadership means that someone has availed himself or herself to be an example of what you are to become if you keep following that person. In biology, if you want to know what you're developing into, all you have to do is look at where you've come from. Most of us look like one or both of our natural parents, or we look like someone in our families. Our predecessors give us a physical snapshot of our futures.

According to evolutionists, you are a creature with no future, no purpose and nothing to evolve into other than a corpse. If you believe this concept, you would have to believe that you are the result of chance; there is nothing purposeful about your existence and there is no assignment attached to your life. It's no wonder this world is full of crazy people! If you've come from an animal, then nature would suggest that you are developing into an animal. This again is a flagrant misrepresentation of who we are, and this is why you can't allow others to define you. As a leader, you need to know who you are; this represents your identity. If you don't know who you are, you will be misrepresented until you figure it out. Misrepresentation can be a dangerous event when you're not mature enough to absorb its impact. Let's compare this to the potter at the wheel. Impact on wet clay leaves an imprint, but as long as the clay is wet, the potter can smooth out the imprint. The potter, of course, represents the mentor. You need people to tell you that you are not an animal, even when you are behaving like one. Otherwise, by the time your countenance hardened, you would be covered with the fingerprints and opinions of broken people.

Procrastination

What type of mold or profile are you creating? Who are you patterning yourself after, and why should your leadership be trusted? What sacrifices have you made for the advancement of your vision? Lastly, if a mold of your character had been created ten years ago, would you still be able to fit into that same mold today or have you outgrown it? Every leader needs to be able to measure the distance between each season of his or her life; this allows the leader to measure his or her growth. Leaders who can't measure their growth are leaders who haven't grown much. What do you call someone who isn't growing? The medical term for this is developmentally delayed. Mental and emotional growth have nothing to do with the size of your brain, they have everything to do with where you are in your perspective versus where you've come from. This growth denotes the measurable amount of distance that you've journeyed from one thought process or mindset to another. For example, a five-year old's mind has made some major advancements and developments from the space of time when the child was a year old versus when he turned five-years old. This is a journey that the child has taken, but not with his feet; he's taken this journey in his mind. If a five-year old boy still talks, reasons and behaves like a year-old boy, psychiatrists and psychologists would say that the child is developmentally delayed, meaning, the child is stuck at a certain stage of development. They would then look at the child's brain and his parents in an attempt to figure out why he isn't developing like a normal child. His developmental delay may not be rooted in a deformation of his brain, it may be the result of poor parenting. Maybe his parents neglected to read to him; maybe his parents have locked him away in a room and he hasn't had many human interactions since his birth. While this is cruel and unusual behavior that signifies that there's something wrong with the parents, we all know that worse events have taken place. This would mean that he has horrible leaders or, at best, no leaders.

Did you know that procrastination, in short, is nothing but a self-inflicted mental, emotional and sometimes even financial delay? It is a form of self-neglect which, of course, is a form of abuse. Yes, we can and do abuse ourselves! It can also serve as a social delay and a psychological delay. This is why timelines are important. As a leader, you need to monitor your growth; you also need to monitor your productivity. If you are procrastinating to read a book or write a book, you are not only hurting yourself, you are hurting the people who follow you or should be following you. Would you intentionally restrict your child's education? Of course, you wouldn't! This would be child neglect which, again, is abuse! The next question is obvious—if you know the power of advancing forward, why would you intentionally hold yourself back? Most people do this, all the while promising themselves that when a specific event occurred in their lives that they would finally do the work needed to advance their missions. This rarely happens. Instead, every New Year's eve, social media is almost shut down by procrastinators making their public declarations regarding what they intend to do in the new year. Hear me on this—procrastination is either a sign of immaturity, rebellion, fear or self-hatred. Nevertheless, every leader comes to a halt at some point, and this is why I keep saying that every leader needs a leader. Your leader will notice when there is no movement in your life, and your leader should address this the minute he or she notices it. Let's look at the Leaders' Spectrum again.

Consumers/ Complainers	Spectators/ Procrastinators	Producers/ Solutionists

As you can see, a procrastinator is a step up from a complainer, but a step behind a producer. Procrastination can be addressed easily when you learn to self-govern. For example, tell your mentor/leader what you are planning to do, hand the leader a blueprint and a date of completion. Take the "I'm doing this for me" mentality out of the equation, and commit the project to your leader. A great example of this is, you've been planning to write a book, but you can't seem to stop procrastinating. To rectify this, type the name of your book on a document and create a table of contents for your book. Also, create a thank you page, thanking your leader for all he or she has done. Send the manuscript to your leader and say, for example, "To show you how much I appreciate your leadership, I am going to publish this book a few days before your birthday." What have you just done? It's called obligation; you've just obligated yourself to a deadline. And to secure that deadline, you have enlisted the help of someone you honor and respect. So now, you are no longer operating in the mentality that you are writing the book to tell your story, you essentially trigger the responsibility mechanism that's in your brain.

True Representation
Rehearse this next line in your mind: "I am an ambassador." What is an ambassador, you ask? In short, an ambassador is a representative of something or someone. Believe it or not, as independent and strong as you may be, you are representing something or someone. You have patterned yourself after someone. Why is this important to note? Because you need to know that there is someone monitoring your choices; that person or that group of people may not necessarily tell you that they are surveying your life, and this is why you have to be mindful of the choices you make, especially if you are leading others or you plan to lead others. This is also important because many of us have patterned our lives after others, and even though we've stopped following these people, we are still following their

patterns. For example, have you ever said something, only to realize that you not only said something someone in your past used to say, but that you said it in their tone? This is because, as humans, we don't just stop patterning ourselves after people when we stop following them. We normally find things that we like about other people and we pattern those behaviors, and while this can be okay, it can also lead us to the very pits that those people have fallen into. What does this mean? It means that we should always be consciously aware of the people we are representing, even if we are no longer fans or followers of theirs. Every leader is like a tree; we must prune ourselves often and monitor the fruit that's being produced in our lives; this will allow us to see what we're representing and who we are representing. We need to know whose mold we are attempting to fit ourselves into. Now, this isn't to say that you can't have flaws. Every good leader is also a flawed leader. Let's go back to the idea of a mold. If we were to create a mold of our faces, that mold would not be smooth; that is, unless the potter smoothed out all of our blemishes, cuts and imperfections. When people look at our faces, they don't see perfection. Your face is the part of you that's always visible for others to see, and your imperfections help others to accept their own imperfections. Most people who've committed suicide did so because they felt alone in their struggles; they felt singled out and hopeless. Our flaws help others to see that perfection is not something any of us can attain. In Hollywood, the men and women are painted with layers and layers of makeup, and their pictures are often photoshopped or airbrushed. This has created an unrealistic standard of beauty within our culture. Nowadays, men and women alike are ripping their faces apart trying to look like the men and women they see on billboards and in magazines. As a leader, you are a mold, but don't be afraid to let your flaws show. Don't model perfection; it's unrealistic and it does more damage than it does good. Of course, you have to be sensitive and wise enough to know when to show off your flaws and to whom you should show your flaws. By being transparent, you have to create a realistic standard for other leaders to follow. Again, you shouldn't be creating photocopies of yourself; instead, you are creating a standard by which other leaders can measure themselves.

By being your flawed self, you create a mold that others can relate to. You also help other leaders to truly represent you whenever they decide to discuss your leadership with other emerging leaders. You were not created to be anything other than yourself! Now, if you are immature and you love rebelling, this isn't to say that you should go out and paint the town red with your choices. No, you need to be seated under a mentor, allowing yourself to be developed. What I'm saying is, learn to represent the person you are designed to be, not who you pretended to be or learned to be along the way. When you reach the level of authenticity, you are ready to create a mold of yourself or a pattern by which other leaders should follow.

Maturing as a Leader
Cambridge Dictionary defines the word "mature" this way

(verb): "to become more developed mentally and emotionally and behave in a responsible way, or to cause someone to do this." To develop simply means to grow. Here, Cambridge talks about developing mentally and emotionally; this means that you have to put yourself in a climate or an atmosphere to receive new information, and your beliefs have to repeatedly be readjusted, not just to accommodate the new information, but to be changed by that information. This, according to Cambridge, has to be done in a responsible way. The word "responsible" has everything to do with how you respond to conflicts, events, seasons and people. For example, a toddler often responds to negative stimuli by crying or throwing a tantrum, but when the child begins to develop and mature more, the child learns to respond in a more mature way. When the child is about three-years old, he starts asking a lot of questions, rather than crying about what he doesn't understand. This is one of the many stages of his development. If the parent answers all of the questions in a way that the child understands, he'll continue to develop mentally and emotionally, slowly becoming the man that he was born to become. He wasn't born to be a cute baby for the rest of his life. He was born to become a responsible man; he was born to become a leader, a solutionist and a mold by which his sons and followers could measure themselves by. He was born to respond to some of the problems that we see today.

"Cover me!" Many of us have sat on the edges of our seats, ground our teeth together and clinched our fists as we've watched our favorite movie characters in the midst of a gun fight. The fight would be intense and the odds would be against them, but our favorite characters were always bold and unfazed by the threat of death. They'd be hiding behind a parked car when they would suddenly yell out those words we love to hate. "Cover me!" Fearing the worst, but hoping for the best, we've all scooted to the edge of our seats and stared intently at our television screens. The good guy would suddenly rise from his hiding place with two guns in his hands—one in each hand, of course. He would then squat and run towards his enemies, using the cars as covers, while his friends and allies stood to their feet and unloaded a series of rounds against their enemies. Our hero would suddenly emerge and fire off a series of shots. We'd leap from our seats whenever he blew something up, despite the fact that he'd been shot himself. The movie would end with him standing in front of an ambulance with a sling on his arm and the evidence of the chaotic gunfight in the background. He'd say something witty, blink his eyes and the film would freeze from there, before playing the credits.

Cover me. Why would a trained assassin ask a bunch of folks who are clearly inferior to him to cover him? This is one of the signs that he has matured as a leader. You see, in the beginning of these types of films, our hero is often an arrogant loner who loves mayhem. A large part of the movie would be about getting him to trust his colleagues enough to involve them on his missions. We'd soon discover why he's rebelled against his leaders; it would often be because someone near and dear to him had been killed in his presence. Still wrestling with the guilt from this person's death, he's in a sense, become somewhat suicidal. His suicidal tendencies, to us, look like boldness. In truth, he simply lost his will to live. This is what made him a dangerous opponent. But his maturity would be evident towards the end. He'd trust his colleagues more and his will to live would clearly have been restored. In an hour and a half, we've watched him go from being a suicidal, destructive and borderline crazy human being to becoming a true leader. And just like we've watched him grow, we need someone to monitor our growth; this way, that person can tell if we're maturing or not.

Below are five signs that you have matured or are maturing as a leader, but again, I can't emphasize this enough—you are NOT qualified to check your own fruit. You need someone who's been where you are trying to go to monitor your development. Here are five signs that you are heading in the right direction:

1. **You have someone to cover you and you submit to that covering.** The reason our hero said, "Cover me" is because he needed his enemies to be distracted while he quietly advanced towards them. Make no mistake about it. Everything that you decide to build will have its fair share of enemies. Some of them will fashion themselves as competitors, some of them may attempt to sue you and some of them will pretend to be your friends. This is why I won't stop

saying that you NEED a mentor!

2. **You've mapped out a plan.** Whether this is a business plan, a blueprint or a family plan, any plan that's been put on paper is a plan in motion.

3. **You have outgrown unrealistic expectations.** This doesn't just include the unrealistic expectations of others, but it deals more with the unrealistic expectations that you have. For example, I pastor a church, so I've seen my fair share of people who've had unrealistic reasoning. People will leave churches for the most shallow reasons. Some folks leave because they think their pastors are supposed to give them their undivided attention and some people leave because their pastors preached a sermon that pricked their hearts. Don't be one of these people! Be realistic in everything you do and in every relationship you have!

4. **You become more solution-minded than you are problem-centered.** As I mentioned earlier, there are going to be people who intentionally and unintentionally misrepresent your character, but you can't put your focus on these people. You have to look for problems that are worthy of your attention and then solve them. As leaders mature, they become less "hater-focused" and more solution-oriented.

5. **Procrastination has quickly become a thing of the past.** Mature or maturing leaders talk less and demonstrate more.

Of course, this is just a short list. Your mentor should be able to measure your development if you stay put and you are transparent with him or her. Maturing as a leader involves a series of events—some pleasant, some unpleasant. Remember, you are climbing a spectrum, going from being a complainer to being a producer. This journey is not without its fair share of obstacles, but every obstacle you face requires a certain amount of maturity to overcome. Keep pressing forward; there are people out there who need you to emerge so that they can have a healthy and clear mold of a leader. Take your time; don't rush the process. Get the healing, the counseling and the information you'll need to become a mature and effective leader.

Homework (Activation)

List three things that you've been procrastinating to do, and then, get the ball rolling. Write out a plan, and submit your plan to your leader. This is going to stretch you. You may feel uncomfortable sharing your vision with anyone, but accountability creates visibility!

Leadership Beliefs

What is leadership? Leadership is the discipline to lead yourself to a destination that inspires others to trust your steps to find their paths to success. Oftentimes, we've been taught that leadership is a task, and I am trying to change the narrative on this idea of leadership being a task, but leadership actually being a person. Leadership is a discipline. It takes discipline to be a leader, and I believe that if you can't lead yourself, you can't lead organizations and you can't lead people. The root word of discipline is "disciple." In other words, discipline requires discipleship. You need to find someone to mentor and instruct you; this is what accelerates your vision.

Another word for discipline is "maturity." Every time you master discipline in a certain area of your life, you've pretty much matured in that area. But consider this; you are like a tree with many branches. Most trees can bear both ripe fruit and unripe fruit at the same time. This is why a farmer will search a tree, finding and picking the ripest fruits and leaving the others on the tree until they are mature enough to be picked. There are parts of you that are mature, just as there are parts of you that are immature. The way that you show that you're actually ready to lead yourself is through discipline; this is the regiment that you have to lead yourself to a desired destination. Discipline is the evidence of maturity. Oftentimes, we have been taught that leadership is about the person who's first, when I have found that there are a lot of people who are first because they are loud and aggressive. They are first because they're loudmouthed or they are the first to speak up, but this does not make them leaders. There are a lot of people who are willing to speak up about things, but they don't lead change. They don't lead any area of influence in their personal lives that show that they are people who are worthy of being followed. People who have more opinions than they have knowledge are bitter fruit. In other words, they aren't ready to be picked; they are not mature enough to lead anyone. I like to say it like this—leadership is showing people the lions, the tigers and the bears that you've slayed, and how you've built a level of discipline to lead yourself to a place that shows other people that you are worth being followed. The fundamental of leadership is when you can lead yourself to a destination.

Leadership is the most necessary component to achieving goals. It is necessary to achieve aspirations, and I believe that leadership is the only way to see dreams fulfilled. I do understand that leadership is complex; there are a lot of organizations that are out teaching the fundamentals of leadership, but I believe that, as complex as leadership is, it is also one of the simplest functions to perform if certain disciplines are understood. I would like to submit to you that leadership is not a task, leadership is a person. It's you! It's you discovering who you are; it's you understanding and leading yourself in a way that people will desire and trust you to lead them! It's you having the discipline to regiment your life, regiment where you're headed, regiment your vision and your mission in a way that leads you to a desired destination and builds into it the trust that people need to have to say, "Hey look, if you can do it, so can I!" This means that leadership involves you discovering who you are! This is your identity.

Often, we've been taught the idea that leadership is just, "Do what I do" or "Do what I say do." I believe that this is because many of us grew up in households witnessing our parents do things that we weren't allowed to do, nor were we expected to do. "I want you to be better than me." We've all heard this. Our parents would often try to lead us with their words, but not through their actions. It didn't take long for them to realize that this type of leadership is rarely effective. Leadership should inspire others to see that they have the potential to do what they desire to do in their lives by watching what you've done for your life. In other words, you have to become a template or a standard. If a mother wants to convince her daughters to honor and respect themselves, she has to honor and respect herself. If a father wants to teach his sons to avoid the wrong crowds, he has to be mindful of the company he keeps. This is because anytime a person has a position of leadership is someone else's life, that person serves as a sample of what the person he's leading has the potential to become. His voice is just the instrument that teaches him how to become what he's seeing. For example, we all love Dr. Myles Munroe. His words were powerful, but his life was even more powerful. Most of us would not be watching his videos or quoting his quotes if his lifestyle didn't line up with his messages. He had to not only practice what he preached, he had to become what he preached. He was a leader in every sense of the word; he didn't just lead people, but he embodied the very heart of a leader.

The word "leadership" can be broken down into two words: leader and ship. You are a vessel. A vessel is a ship or a large boat. Vessels are designed to transport goods from one place to another; this means that something valuable is inside you. But unlike a ship, your journey isn't about getting you to a physical location. Your journey is about changing your mind, not just about yourself, but about the world at large. You are the captain of your leader-ship. Your assignment is to steer yourself—mind, body and soul—into a better mindset. This has nothing to do with your abilities; it has everything to do with your belief system. You see, if your beliefs change, so will your behavior. Your beliefs are the fuel that drives your behavior.

I want you to imagine a large vessel, and inside of that vessel, I want you to image a room full of potted apple trees. The vessel is supposed to arrive in China six years from today—the exact amount of time needed for the trees to grow up and began bearing fruit. The buyers have made it clear that they are willing to pay a lot of money for these trees, but only if they are bearing fruit. The fruit is the evidence that the trees are healthy. You dock the ship and use it as a greenhouse for several years. Over the years, many storms have come and the boat has struggled to stay put. On five occasions, the anchor broke and the ship went off to sea midways through a storm, but you were able to recover it and place a new anchor on it. You finally got tired of nearly losing your ship at sea, so you went ahead and invested in an expensive anchor, one that is guaranteed to not break. All the same, you have maintained a certain atmosphere on the boat in order for the plants to grow, so there are certain regions that you simply can't go into. There are even times when you're desperately in need of the money that the buyers have promised you, but the fruit on the ship was not ready. There was a lot that you wanted to do, but your responsibility and your vision helped to keep you ashore.

The water from the ocean is salty, so you couldn't use it to water the trees. This was frustrating because that water was readily available to you, but you had to travel near and far to get fresh water for your trees almost everyday. The more the trees began to grow, the more you realized that the pots they were in would never allow them to grow to their full potential. They needed height and depth; they needed space to grow. So, over the years, you've had to re-pot the trees many times. Your friends said that you were crazy. Your family mocked and scorned you. Before long, you found yourself questioning whether or not you should continue watering and pruning the trees aboard the ship. And because of the many storms, the ship began to look weathered and beaten, nevertheless, the ship remained valuable because of what was in it. Other sailors ridiculed you as they took their boats out on the water.

Every time you watered or pruned one of the trees, you were giving it the equivalent of knowledge, and every time you brought the trees on the deck to receive sunlight, you allowed the branches to receive revelation. One day, it finally happened. The trees started bearing fruit. China was just a two-week journey away by boat, so you hopped aboard and started your journey. Once you arrived at your destination, the buyers were there to examine the fruit. "These are delicious," one buyer said in a strong Mandarin accent. The buyer then hands you a large check and unloads all of the fruits from your vessel, but to your surprise, the buyer doesn't take the trees. The reason for this, according to him, was because the trees could not grow in his environment, so he told you to take the trees with you and continue to grow more fruit. Of course, he was going to pay you every time you had a harvest. This gave you the ability to bear more fruit and return to China every time harvest season came around. Other nations even started calling you because the fruit you bore was one of a kind. This is a picture of leadership; this is a picture of you! You are the ship and what's in you is invaluable. The people who need what you have are your buyers, and while they may not be exchanging money for revelation, they are giving life to your mission. Again, all of these fruits have stages, and every stage represents your belief system. What you believe will always be expressed in your words and your choices. What you believe will impact your leadership and the people who follow you.

Leadership really needs a fresh perspective because it's been sold with a lot of lofty ideas. It is for this reason that most people feel like it's impossible to obtain leadership. The "regular Joe" feels like he can't become a leader because he thinks it's meant for the lofty people, the smart people or the gifted people. Leadership is the discipline to lead yourself to a desired destination that inspires others to trust your steps to find their own paths to success. Think about it this way. Have you ever gone hiking? If you have, you'll notice that they've placed certain markers around the campsite; these markers are designed to help you find your way back out of the wilderness should you get lost. These markers are very similar to leaders; they all point you towards the exit of one season and the entrance of another. They keep you from getting lost in the wilderness when you're starting your hike, and they keep you from going too deep into the wilderness once you've become comfortable. Additionally, you'll find signs throughout the campsites that point you to certain destinations. This means that they've accepted the responsibility to lead you. Why is this important to note? Because immaturity will lead you to believe that people are obligated to mentor or lead you, when they are not. Like I mentioned earlier, I've come across my fair share of people with unrealistic expectations and unsound reasoning, and of course, this only meant that their immaturity was on display. When someone accepts the responsibility of mentoring you, be grateful, not entitled. You have to then take on the responsibility of being honest and available. Remember, your leader does not work on your time table.

Responsibility is a compound word; it's "response" and "ability." It's the ability to respond, but maturity is the ability to respond correctly. So leadership requires a person to have the confidence to respond to problems in a timely manner and the maturity to give the correct response. Leadership is your way of saying that you have a problem and you've decided to personally take the responsibility of solving that problem. Every business is nothing but a set of problems being solved. McDonald's solves the problem of hunger; when your car is broken, your car mechanic solves that problem, and when your hair is unkempt, your barber or beautician solves that problem. The truth of the matter is, institutions are built on solving problems. That's what leadership is. Leadership, at its root, is a problem-solving entity. It is a person who says, "Look, I have the discipline to have led my life to a place of freedom; this gives me the ability to respond to problems that are in our world." We can't walk in the fullness of our leadership capacity if we don't deal with our belief systems, because there are so many people out there trying to do leadership, instead of trying to be leaders; they are trying to do leadership, instead of realizing that leadership is a being. It is the essence of who we are. For example, I am not trying to assume the responsibilities of a leader. I am a leader and I am responsible. This means that, while I am on a journey, I also serve as a map to others. People don't follow my feet, they follow my example. I am a runway model; I model the mindset that I want others to wear, but I also have to return to the dressing room to allow my mind to continually be changed. As I grow into each one of these mindsets, I'll come out of my dressing room to model those mindsets for others. The same is true for you.

There are some beliefs that you have to understand to walk in leadership.

1. You have to believe in yourself.
2. You must have passion.
3. You must love people.
4. You must be free from the opinions of people.
5. You have to live for the betterment of others.

You have to believe in yourself. Why is this important? Many of us, especially African-Americans, have been struggling with a demon I call the demon of self-devaluation. It's a demon that we have been dealing with since oppression. Oppression has caused us to diminish our beliefs regarding our ability to make change in our world. You have to believe in yourself. This isn't the elementary idea that you can be what you want to be. Yes, you can, but what I'm saying is, you have to tackle the demon of self-devaluation—the demon that many of us have defined and disguised as humility. It is the idea that we are diminishing our ability to see who we truly are, who the world needs us to be and who we have the potential to become. Let me help you with this. Do you know that God is not surprised or scratching His head about the problems in this world? God is not concerned about the problems in this world because He put you in the world. Think about this. God put you in this world with the gifts, the skill-sets and the abilities that you have because the problems in this world were meant to be confronted by a person like you! God decided that you would be the solution to these problems; you are the ship that God has designed to lead yourself and then others! The Earth is the Lord's and the fullness thereof; God knew the condition this world would be in right now before He created you. God's not concerned with the problems that are in this world, after all, He put you in the world at this time because He knows you have the ability to make change, but will you take the responsibility to make these changes? So, you have to believe in yourself. We have this demon of self-devaluation because we have devalued our abilities and we have devalued ourselves. And to add insult to injury, we are calling this humility when it's truly humiliating. So, a lot of us are not operating in our full capacities because we think we're going to do too much. The truth of the matter is, that's not how we were designed to respond. Let me give you a mental picture.

I can look and see a sign with a speed limit on it. The speed limit can be forty miles per hour. This means that I'm not breaking the law until I drive forty-one miles per hour. I'm not breaking the law if I'm driving forty miles per hour, nor am I rewarded if I drive 34 miles per hour when the speed limit is forty. What I'm saying is, so many of us living our lives at 34 miles per hour, when we should have our feet on the gas, and we should be living our lives at forty. That's what I mean by self-devaluation. We are living under such an oppressive mentality that we have been taught that being first is evil, being a leader is evil and having nice things is evil; and because we've been taught this, a lot of us are not living in our full capacity. We think that we are going to err over on the side of pride. Here is the truth about pride. Pride means to have a closed perspective. Pride is when you say that there's no need for anymore information to come into your life. Humility is not thinking of yourself less; humility is understanding your ability and not allowing yourself to think that you have all the information to better yourself. Humility is understanding your abilities and your capacity, but not capping off your mentality because you think you don't need anymore information to help you become better. Pride is a closed perspective. Humility is understanding yourself properly. Let's revisit the concept of the ship. Pride is knowing that your trees need to be watered, but refusing to let anyone water them because you are worried about how this would make you look in the eyes of your peers. Humility is opening the door and letting those people on, regardless of what others will say. Humility is not self-devaluation; this is why we in the church have to really deal with this mentality. A lot of us have devalued ourselves because we don't think we are valuable enough to sit at certain tables or be in certain rooms. We don't think we're valuable enough to live in certain places, drive certain vehicles or make a certain amount of money because we've been taught that if we reach for the stars, we're doing too much. This mentality has to be broken in order for you to operate in a level of incredible leadership. Believing in yourself is imperative. Really understanding this means to deal with the spirit of self-oppression or self-devaluation.

You need to survey the traumas of your past, because whenever you don't survey the trauma, you will lead through that filter. That will be the filter by which you make decisions and the filter by which you relate to others. If you've been hurt, you will process life and process your leadership decisions through your hurt. This is what a lot of us have been dealing with; this is why many of us are unable to be level-headed and clear about making leadership decisions and being influencers. A lot of us are dealing with trauma and we're trying to define this trauma as our personalities when the truth is, we've been hurt. Hurt has become the filter in which we gauge our decisions as leaders. You don't want to diminish the quality of your leadership because you're processing decisions through your pain. Your pain shouldn't define you and you shouldn't define your leadership by your pain; instead, your pain should refine you. It is the furnace by which you were tried.

Again, you have to believe in yourself. And while this sounds elementary, but you have to deal with the demon of self-devaluation. You have to deal with the demon of oppression. We have been taught things that have systematically made us feel that we are unworthy of making decisions that would move humanity forward. I'm here to tell you that the reason you're here today is because you have the ability to respond correctly.

You must have passion. It sounds simple, but let's dig into it. Your passion is not about what you're willing to die for, your passion is shown through what you're willing to live for. Oftentimes, we've been taught that passion is what we are willing to die for, and I understand this, but I want you to understand that passion is shown in what you're willing to live for. The reason that you have to have passion in leadership is because you will face adversity that will make you say that it's not worth it. Adversity will make you say that it's not worth pressing forward, it's not worth pulling organizations such as your church, your nonprofit organization or your business through the difficulties of dealing with systems and a society that does not always champion good. My question to you is, do you have enough passion to live for what you believe in? Passion ignites a fire in us to fight for what we believe in and stops us from giving up when things are difficult. So, my question isn't what you're willing to die for; my question is, what are you willing to live for? Do you have the passion to keep living to see what's in your heart, in your church or in your organization continue to grow and thrive?

You must love people. We are living in a very interesting day where people want to be on top because they want to be esteemed and celebrated. Your ability or inability to love others has to do with your motives. For leadership to be effective, your motives have to be clear and they have to be pure. You have to love people! I grew up in an environment where a lot of people were preachers, teachers and leaders. They were all of that because of their gift-sets, but not because they really cared about the people, so if they were preaching a sermon, they were preaching it for themselves— not to help the people. Or if they were building organizations, auxiliaries, departments, they built it for themselves, and not for the benefit of the people. In leadership, your motives are important; not having the correct motives caps your ability to respond to problems correctly. Society needs people who really care about the playgrounds of life. What I mean is, there is a quality of life that we're designed to have, but if I'm selfish and self-serving, my quality of life would mean more to me than yours. If we're going to have effective leadership, we need people to care about the overall quality of life for mankind, not just themselves. Does your leadership care only about your comfort or does it care about moving society forward? Again, God's not scratching His head about the problems that are going on in society. That's why you and I are in the Earth. God has His answer. His answer to this world's problems is you and I! If we don't have proper and correct motives toward people, this will stunt our leadership,. There are a lot of people who are really self-centered and insecure. These people use leadership as a way to lord themselves over people, instead of leading organizations and leading people to change—instead of showing other people that they have the possibility and the potential to lead better lives.

You must be free from the opinions of people. When you are a leader, you are taking organizations, you are taking your business, you're taking corporations and you are taking departments into places they've never seen before. People are going to naturally have questions and they are going to naturally misunderstand you. You have to be free from the opinions of people. In leadership, you cannot have soft skin; you have to be tough. You have to understand that people will constantly criticize anything that is new, anything that is unfamiliar and anything that does not look like what they're used to. People are hard-wired for negativity, so in leadership, you have to be bold and you have to remain positive. This is why self-investment is important because when you invest in yourself, you give yourself the armor, the faith and the tenacity that you'll need to be a good leader. It's hard for you to expect people to see what they've never seen before. Leadership is an art. What we're doing is, taking something that is invisible, something that is in another realm, and we're bringing it into reality or man's realm. So, you're dealing with people who've never seen what you've seen, so oftentimes, their skepticism has nothing to do with them not liking or believing in you; they're skeptical because they've never seen anyone do what you're trying to do. In other words, they lack faith.

You have to be free from the opinions of people; you have to understand that it is always lonely at the top. You cannot expect to be understood. You can't look for people to understand your moves; you can't expect people to understand why you make certain decisions because they can't see it. In leadership, what we're striving to do is take what's in our heads and make it a reality. We're taking vision and making it a reality. This is the finesse of leadership because we're taking something that is unseen and making it real to people, and we're making it seen in a way that benefits and impacts their lives for the better. This is why I urge you to deal with your trauma and deal with your triggers; you can't be a person who wears your feelings and emotions on your shoulders in leadership. You can't be a vengeful person; you can't be a person who's okay with pettiness and drama. Because what it does is diminishes your value in leadership and it diminishes people's respect for your voice. In leadership, you have to be okay with being a person who is standing alone. You have to know how to hold yourself together emotionally. The reason we're having such a difficult time in society right now with leadership is because we really have people who are leading with traumas that have not been dealt with, so oftentimes, their gifts take them to places that their character wasn't ready for. I know this is a common statement, but I want to break the word character down for you.

Oftentimes, we have defined character to mean a person's behavior when, honestly, it's a little deeper than that.

Character comes from the root concept of statue. If you know anything about a statue, you should know that a statue is beat into shape using pressure and fire. Once it's molded into shape, I can sit that statue outside, and that statue can weather the storms—regardless of whether it's raining or hailing, that statue remains the same. So, character is developed over the course of time. Character and reputation are two totally different things. In church, when we're saying that a person is a person of character, we're misdiagnosing some people. We've all had seasons in our lives when we haven't done everything right—we've had seasons where we haven't been behaviorally or morally right. We've done things that weren't right even when our hearts and our intentions were good. Our motives were to do the right thing, but we were in the process of molding our character. So, understand why this is important in leadership, because the self-investment and the self-development that we're doing is molding our character and building the discipline into us that becomes the things that are unmovable about us. What's unmovable about me? My heart towards people! This is because I've dealt with the traumas I've had to deal with concerning people in my life, so now, I have a value for people that allows me to deal with hard and snippy people because I know that they're in a place of immaturity. Character is important because it is something that is built over time. The truth is, we don't know if a person is at the pinnacle of their character until that person dies. Because character is something that is always being formed. This should bring great joy to you because you may have had areas in your life that have been difficult or you may have been out of shape, but those things can be reshaped through your repentance and your development. So, character is something that is seen over time; this is important. This is why you have to self-invest in mentors who put pressure on you because that's how you get shaped.

Reputation is very different. Reputation is how other people view you. That is important in leadership as well. If you do the hard work on your character, your character will take care of your reputation. But if you do the hard work on your reputation without taking care of your character, you will become a plastic leader. That's what we're dealing with today! We're dealing with people who are plastic! They don't do the hard work behind the scenes; they only do the work on their reputations, so they only work on perceptions. That's why there are a lot of leaders setting up photo shoots and everybody's coming out with a flyer; think about it. Everyone's trying to do the work on their reputations because they're trying to craft a narrative by which people relate to them based on people's perceptions of them. But if you do the harder work on your character, which is more behind-the-scenes works—it's the internal work that you're doing on your heart and your disciplines—what it does is superimposes itself on your reputation. This is super important in the conversation of leadership because oftentimes, we think that being first is being perfect when the truth of the matter is, being first means that I'm the first to change; it means that I'm doing the work on myself to make sure that I'm healthy emotionally, physically and intellectually. I'm doing the to work to ensure that whenever I'm making decisions for churches, organizations and businesses, I'm doing it all with purpose. I'm doing it to make a meaningful change and a meaningful impact on the lives of people because I did the soulish work, not just work on my reputation. I wanted to dig into that point before we moved on to the next pointer, because we've been taught somethings about leadership— we've been taught misconceptions that I'm finding that many people have been imprisoned by. They don't feel like God can use them because they have flaws; we all have flaws! There's not one person on the planet who's leading any organization that does not have flaws, but you have to stay under somebody's pressure to ensure that your flaws are addressed. Pressure is the force that frames you.

There are things in my past that have hurt me, and I've allowed them to be a part of my mentality and how I lead because I've had some experiences in leadership and in my personal life that have negatively impacted me. Those experiences have taught me how to treat people better. I think this is why I'm more compassionate towards people because I've been on the abusive side of leadership, so I know the pain and what that can do to people. I'm more flexible in my church's structure because I've experienced abuse. From the simplistic standpoint, I've experienced things that have made me intentional about how I structure particular things to help people.

You have to live for the betterment of others. This is called sacrifice. If you are going to be an impactful leader, you have to live free from corruption. This is why your motives are important. The Bible tells us to present our bodies as a living sacrifice, holy and acceptable unto God, which is our reasonable service. I believe that what a lot of people are doing is only presenting their bodies as alive sacrifices, meaning, they're not living. Living a full life is important to your leadership abilities, because how can you lead change in organizations, societies, departments or people when you have not lived a full life? This is why you have to deal with oppression. You have to deal with mental oppression, financial oppression and emotional oppression, just to name a few. This is because your worldview impacts your ability to make correct leadership decisions. This is why the Bible says that Jesus came that we may have life, and we may have life more abundantly. Notice, He did not say that He came so that we could have church, and church more abundantly. I'm making this point specific because a lot of us are framing our leadership within the context of a church service when the world is way bigger than our little church services; it's way bigger than the church that I pastor. So, I don't process leadership from a church service standpoint. I have to live a full life so that this can impact my ability to make very big decisions for organizations. This is why I'm saying that you have to live a free life. Live free from a system that causes you to be oppressed.

How do you build your self-worth without becoming prideful?

My answer is self-investment, and making sure that you're healthy physically, emotionally and intellectually. These are your checks and your balances. What happens is, you have to create more value in yourself through investing in yourself. The Bible tells us to be fruitful and to multiply. Notice that it did not tell us to be seedful. This is a powerful statement because it means that in order for us to be fruitful, the seeds are already on the inside of us. If we want to be fruitful, we have to water the seeds. This is what I mean by self-investment. I believe that self-care and self-leisure are parts of self-investment, but I also believe that you have to do the hard work of self-stimulation through reading books and making sure that you are watering the seeds that are on the inside of you. Self-investment is important—going to the gym, reading, exposing yourself to new information and submitting yourself to qualitative mentorship. These all allow you the ability to grow yourself. If you don't know the fullness of yourself, you don't know when to pull back. There are a lot of people who say that they are humble when the truth is, you can't be humble if you don't know yourself. Most of us only know where we're bad; a lot of us don't know where we're good. Most of us only know what we don't do well; most of us don't know what we do well because we think that self-celebration is pride. Self-celebration is a sign of maturity; expecting other people to celebrate you is a sign of immaturity. I have to be aware of my abilities and my capacities in order to know when to dial it back. If I don't want to err into pride, I have to know the fullness of my abilities. In order for me to know that I'm breaking the speed limit, I have to know the speed limit. But here's the problem. The speed limit is different in America than it is on the Autobahn. On the Autobahn, you can drive 190 miles per hour, but in America, you can only drive thirty, forty or fifty miles per hour. What I'm saying is, a lot of us have limited our leadership and our world views because we're being told that we're doing too much when the truth of the matter is, we haven't fully understood the fullness of ourselves yet to even gauge the definitions of pride versus humility. We don't know our capacities and our own abilities. You haven't even lived on the Autobahn of life yet to know that you're doing too much. So, self-celebration is a sign of maturity, but expecting everyone else to celebrate you is a sign of immaturity.

I launched my church because I saw that there were a lot of people who were tired of church, as usual; they were tired of religious churches. Religious churches were based on what you did in church, not who you were. They based your value on if you had a title in church, whether you preached or taught in church—it wasn't really built on whether you had a relationship with God. It was more about what you did for the church. I saw that they weren't helping people to build relationships with God or helping them to better understand their dominion mandates. I started this church in response to that problem. I knew that there were people like myself who were tired of churchianity—just going to church and doing church, but not really seeing transformation. This led me on a journey to start a movement to gather a group of people who felt the way I felt. This is how Equation Church was born. There are a lot of problems in society that need people to look at and say, "Hey, that could be better!" I have learned that you have to build out plans to make change. Leadership is about making the quality of life great for all people, not just your favorite people; that's the benefit of leadership.

How do we assert personal development into who we are? Self-investment. If you don't do the hard work of investing in yourself, then you won't be able to understand your fruit. This is important because there are a lot of people who are reading or doing things in life to give out, but not to feed themselves. When you start to feed yourself, you become aware of your gifts, your skill-sets, your abilities and your passions. You have to be aware of these things to actually know where you're called in those areas to lead others.

Who are you? If you can't lead yourself, how can you lead others? Your challenge is to craft a mission statement and ask yourself, "Who am I?" If you don't have any self-awareness, if you don't understand who you are, you won't be able to lead other people.

Homework (Activation)
Write a Mission Statement

Your mission statement needs to become a part of who you are because it will eventually begin to drive you. For example, when I started with my own personal mission statement, I went through several refinements because the more I started to write my mission statements down to sentences that I was able to encapsulate and believe, it started to show me more of who I am. So, when someone asks you, "Who are you?" or "What's your mission in life?" you'll be able to know and articulate to that person who you are.

Maturing in Your Personal Beliefs

Just to recap our last chapter:

1. **You must believe in yourself.** This isn't the elementary "believe in yourself" statement. This means you have to deal with the demons of oppression and self-devaluation. It is ensuring that, in leadership, you have addressed your pain and you have addressed where oppression in your life has played a part in impacting your soul. If you don't deal with pain, what will happen is, you will lead with the filter of your pain. I'm sure you have a few people who come to your mind when we're discussing this. These are the people who appear to be bold or maybe they speak louder than everyone else, but you know that they have some pain that hasn't been dealt with, and so oftentimes, their decisions are made through the filter of their pain. So, it's almost as if their decisions are self-serving, and not about other people, organizations or moving the world forward; it's about their own self-preservation. You have to believe in yourself and again, deal with oppression and self-devaluation. Humility is not thinking less of yourself, it's you knowing your capacities and abilities, which makes you powerful in leadership.

2. **You must passion.** Again, passion is not what you're

willing to die for, it's what you're willing to live for. This is about showing your ability to persevere. In leadership, you need perseverance. You need to push through your obstacles, and you can't give up when people reject you or when people don't necessarily agree with the decisions that you make. Passion has to push you to live for those things that you believe in.

3. **You must love people.** This keeps your motives in check. I know a lot of people who are in positions of authority, but they don't really care about people; they use their positions to give themselves a pat on the back. Loving people is the motive by which we lead. We want to see people become better, we want to see our families become better, we want to see our churches become better and we want to see the world change as a result of our leadership, so again, we must love people.

4. **You have to be free from the opinions of people.** This is basically about you not allowing the opinions of people to control and manipulate your decisions. You have to be free from how people feel and think about you because when you're free from the opinions of people, you'll make quality and sound decisions that aren't motivated by fear.

5. **You must live for the betterment of others.** This means to be free from corruption. So, what you're essentially doing is making sure that, in your leadership, you're allowing yourself to be free, to be pure and to be unspotted from ideas, positions,

money, or anything that will corrupt your ability to make impactful decisions regarding people.

This is just a quick overview of the previous chapter. Of course, there are more, but those are just the fundamental belief systems that you have to have if you're going to be effective in leadership.

Destiny is not a destination. Destiny is a person. Think about it like this—people are going to stand before God, and they're going to say, "I cast out devils in Your Name, I healed the sick in Your Name, I preached the gospel in Your Name," but God is going to say, "Depart from Me, because I never knew you!" In short, He's saying, "I don't know you! I don't have any knowledge of you! When you came back to Me, you looked strange! You didn't look the person I put in the Earth! You don't look familiar to Me!" So, understand why this is important. The whole goal of life is maturity. God will take you on journeys throughout your life, for example, He led Abram to Abraham. He told Abram, "Leave this place and go to a place that I'm going to show you." But he never got to the place because the journey was about revealing to him that he was Abraham; it was never about the place. I want you to realize why this is significant in you developing and maturing in your personal leadership. God uses life to show you yourself. He uses life to teach you the reality of who you are; this is why you have to deal with your pain. If you don't deal with your pain, you will take your life as if it's against you when you have to realize that God is your biggest cheerleader. He's using your life as an obstacle course to reveal you to yourself.

Maturity is what gives you the authority and the insight to manage your life and create a path for others to follow. In management, there has to be self-awareness and there has to be the ability for people and organizations to say that we truly know our gifts, our skill-sets and our capacities; this is what allows us to walk in authority in a specific area. The goal is maturity; this is significant because it breaks fear and it breaks the lack of confidence. When you truly know that you can grow into the person who God has created you to be, you can live where you want to live, drive what you want to drive, eat what you want to eat and go where you want to go. You won't have to leave all of these things up for moral discussion anymore. You won't have to always ask God; instead, you'll learn to be a leader. Leaders make decisions! Again, the goal is maturity; the goal is the measure and the stature of the fullness of a man. What the Bible calls maturity means to look like Jesus. That looks like spiritual maturity—understanding that being a spirit is an identity; it's not a behavior. Being spiritual is not about doing spiritual things; being spiritual is about your identity. You are a spirit put in a body and you possess a soul. So, when you came from Heaven to Earth, you came as a spirit and you were put in a body with a soul.

Oftentimes, people think that growing spiritually is doing spiritual things, when that's not how we grow. The Bible says that the answer to the works of the flesh is the fruit of the Spirit (see Galatians 5). The answer to the works of the flesh: lasciviousness, pride and all of those issues are the fruit of the Spirit. So, if we're trying to grow the fruit of the Spirit, this could only mean that we have the seeds of the Spirit on the inside of us. You water seeds to get fruit. This is how you mature seeds. You put them in the ground, you water them and the seeds have to die; this is the mysterious part of death, and from there, those seeds cause breakthrough in our lives. The fruits of the Spirit are love, joy, peace, patience, kindness, goodness, faithfulness, gentleness and self-control. The fast track to growth is really just perfecting your love walk, which includes love, joy, peace, patience, kindness, goodness, faithfulness, gentleness and self-control. If you learn how to grow in what I call the spiritual emotional fruit, and you learn how to mature your fruit, you will mature. Some of us are trying to obtain maturity through behaviorial modification, but I want you to understand that you have to focus more on creating the fruit of the Spirit.

Below are five points in maturing in your personal leadership:

1. **You have to have an awareness of your identity.** If you don't know who you are, you will never be able to regulate what you do. The problem we're having in leadership today is, we have a lot of people leading without knowing who they are. So, they're trying to do leadership outside of an awareness of who they are in

leadership. So, oftentimes, people think that leadership is just a task; they identify themselves as leaders in certain departments on their jobs, as leaders in their churches or as leaders in their homes. In other words, they think it's task-oriented, when the truth of the matter is, leadership is an identity behavior. It is me leading because I am aware of who I am. When I have self-awareness, what this does is gives me mastery over myself, but if I don't have self-awareness, I won't have mastery or control. The Bible calls this self-control, which is a fruit of the Spirit. Think of the fruit of the Spirit like this—you have love and self-control; they are the bookends. So, love is the motive by which you operate in the fruit of the Spirit and self-control is the behavior. Notice it didn't say God-control. I'm always perplexed by that because the Bible says that if the fruits of the Spirit are in you, it's not that God controls you, it simply means that you have self-control or control over yourself. Again, love is the motive and self-control is the behavior; between these two are the actual behaviors by which you see people operating in spiritual maturity. Oftentimes, in leadership, people think you have to be the first, the top, the biggest, the strongest or the smartest, and I've found that this is not true. Why is it that a lion is called the king of the animal kingdom? It's a big cat! Think about it. A lion is nothing but an overgrown cat, but if an elephant sees a lion, the elephant knows that it's about to be eaten for lunch. A lion sees an elephant and knows that it's getting ready to have lunch. An elephant runs from a cat; a cat runs toward an elephant! Now, the lion isn't the smartest animal—it isn't the fastest, it isn't the biggest, nor is it the strongest. But what is it in a lion that will cause the beast to attack an elephant and think that it can have the elephant for lunch? The answer is a single word. It's called "attitude." We call it mentality, but it's called attitude. You have to realize that, in leadership, the way that you perceive who you are will show up in the quality of your decisions because that lion is aware of its strength and its pace; it's self-aware enough to attack an elephant because an elephant has only been trained to use its size and not its intellect. Because of this, it will run from a lion. This is the difference between many of us because there are a lot of people who choose to have an attitude of who they are; this gives them their authority to operate in leadership. If I don't have a proper awareness of who I am in my abilities, I won't attack problems; instead, I'll run from them. Attitude is important in leadership. This is why I'm talking about an awareness of your identity. Oftentimes, people don't have the leadership attitude or, better yet, the acumen of a right perspective that allows them to be able to attack problems and make changes. Leadership is about making changes; it's about taking institutions and families to a destination. This is why leadership is about, first of all, leading yourself to a destination, because if you don't have the discipline to lead yourself to a destination, then you won't have the discipline to lead other institutions and other people to inspire themselves. Attitude is important and the awareness of your identity is significant. I believe that Satan's number one tool is not demonic possession; I believe that Satan's favorite tool is ignorance. If he can keep you ignorant, he can keep you stuck. Of course, I believe in deliverance and I believe in spiritual warfare, but if you are not transformed by the renewing of your mind, your deliverance is short-lived. The Bible even says that you can go in the house and sweep it clean, but if you don't replace it with information, the devil will come back with stronger ignorance. I'm telling you that Satan's biggest weapon against the people of God is the ignorance of who they are. Many people are involved in what I call churchianity, not Kingdom living. They have no awareness of who they are. They define themselves by their church titles and their skill-sets, instead of understanding that there's much more to them than meets the eye.

2. **The secret to growth is knowledge.** You cannot believe beyond your knowledge. This is significant because a lot of people claim to be believing God for one thing or another, but they won't do the hard work of signing up for mentorship. They won't do the hard work of going to conferences; they won't do the hard work of going to extra-curricular opportunities, going

to college or picking up books, so oftentimes, their beliefs are capped at their knowledge-base. If you're going to mature in your leadership, the secret to doing so is maturing in your knowledge-base. Doing things like reading this book is significant because it's expanding your wineskin. Can I be honest with you? It is knowledge that breaks fear because I don't have to be concerned about my next step if I know what it is! Many people who are afraid to make decisions are that way because they lack knowledge. You have to be a person who loves knowledge if you want to mature in your personal leadership. People who get bored easily when ingesting new information will be locked out of the richness of life. They will be locked out of opportunities; organizations and churches won't be able to trust them because, for example, if I were to put you in a leadership position, what reservoir are you pulling from? How can I trust your decisions if I don't know what reservoir you're sourcing from? What gives your decisions subjectivity? What gives you the authority to say that the carpet should be red versus blue? What gives you the authority to determine the start time or how we invest our money? What gives you the authority to make decisions regarding assets and lives? Oftentimes, the reason so many people aren't trusted enough to be promoted to leadership roles is because there is no validity of their knowledge-base. I can't take someone serious if the information that the person leads from is unaccredited. I know a lot of people who have honorary doctorate degrees that were not earned. There's nothing worse than spending money on a degree that is unaccredited. This means that the paper carries no weight! They have the title, but they don't have the real authority to be a leader in certain areas because they didn't earn the degrees or the institutions that taught them the information aren't accredited. What I'm saying is, it can be difficult for people to trust your leadership and your decisions if your knowledge-base is centered around how you feel, and you don't have any validation or accreditation that gives any weight to your voice or your thoughts.

3. **People are living resources.** Listen to and watch people. Most of the time when I enter a room, I'm typically the quietest person in the room. I have learned a lot from people-watching. What I'm doing is soaking up conversations and I'm listening. I've learned that people are living resources, so if you're going to mature in your leadership, you're going to have to put yourself in positions that make you uncomfortable and to put yourself in positions where you are not the authority, so that you can continue to grow. You have to put yourself in places with people who may have been exposed to more information— people who have a higher degree of leadership capacity or winds under their belts. This gives you the exposure that you need to continue to learn. Don't be

a person who's reclusive, because if you are, you can miss out on critical information. I love being at home and I love being by myself because I'm an only child, so I don't necessarily always need to be around people, but I know that if I need particular information, I know how to get on a flight or pick up the phone—I know how to invite somebody to lunch or dinner and just give them the green light to talk while I listen. Some people have experiences that can fast track you and mature you in your leadership. Some people are living resources, so deal with your hurt so that you're not suspicious of everybody.

4. **Value books.** I'll be honest with you. It's what you receive from the book that determines the value of the book itself. There are a lot of people who brag about having books, but they don't necessarily extract any information from the books. The value of the book is what you actually receive from it. There are seasons when I need specific information, so I'll pick up a book, read it and I'll extract the information that I need from it; this is when the book becomes valuable to me. There are some books that I read every year because the more I dig into those books, the more I see what I didn't see the first few times I read it. There are some books that I read because they intellectually stimulate me and they help me with information that I want to unpack or learn. The point of this is to educate yourself. Pick up and read books. I'm not saying that you have to be a book nerd, but the more you're

willing to read, ingest and take in, the better the quality of your decisions will be. This is because you now have a wealth of information that you're pulling from. Who wants to be in an organization, church or family that has limited resources and information? Nobody wants to be led by someone who's making decisions based on how that person feels! I know a lot of people who are married to uninformed leaders and I know a lot of people who are submitted to uniformed leaders. Oftentimes, we call this unsubjective or Spirit-led, but even Spirit-led folks are led back to books; it leads you back to scripture! Spirit-led doesn't mean to pull it out of the sky; it means that you're led back to the scriptures. It leads you back to something that is written because of the authority of paper.

5. **Fail, fail and fail!** Let me tell you a secret to maturing your personal leadership that not many people know. When you fail, this gives the leadership or authority in your life the ability to correct you or to instruct you. What is awesome about failure is when you value correction; this strengthens, grows and matures you. Because a lot of us have come from abusive situations, our first memories of correction are painful; to us, it means we're getting hit physically when this is not true. So, spread your leadership wings by making mistakes, because when you do this, you move from knowledge to wisdom. Knowledge is information, but wisdom is the application of that information. Wisdom is having a wise-dome; it's the love of philosophy or

the love of wisdom. It's really you saying that you're going to move your life from having a bunch of information in your head to moving yourself to a place of wisdom. This is when you're able to operate in a level of leadership that people now trust—they trust your decisions, they trust your voice and they trust your insight because you are now a person of wisdom, not just a person who wants to get your way.

Knowledge. I believe that the real fight is between light and darkness. The cosmic conflict between the kingdoms is light and darkness. Light is revelation; darkness is ignorance. The more people are educated, the more they come out of darkness. The Bible says that you are a royal priesthood, a chosen generation, a peculiar people that will show forth the praises of Him that brought you out of darkness and into His marvelous light. So, the space between getting from darkness to light is education. The more information I get, the more the light bulb comes on about who I am, what my mission is, and the purpose for my life—this breaks fear, procrastination and doubt.

As humans, do we really know what makes us distinct? Do you know what your distinctive is as a human? It's your brain. Geese have to fly South every winter because they cannot control the way they are programmed to think. Every year when it gets cold, they are flying South; there is a great migration of birds because they don't have any control over their intuition. So, what God did for us was to make us in His image and His likeness, and He gave us literal control over our intuition. For this reason, we are able to make decisions that put our lives in varying places; this means that I can survive in the winter, just as I can survive in the heat of summer. I can survive with food and I can survive without food. He's made us so distinctive in the way that we think that we are literally able to conquer any issue that is in our lives. This means that our lives are never stuck. The devil does not have authority over you in any way, shape or form! Because you can't rebuke anything you don't have authority over. You can't cast out something if you don't have authority over it. A police officer can't just put cuffs on me; the only way he can is because he's been given more civil authority, so you can only bind, arrest and cast out what you have authority over. The goal is to get Satan out of our minds and to get him under our feet. This is why I place emphasis on education and its importance because the more you get information and knowledge, the more you'll come to the awareness of yourself, the more you'll be able to operate in strength and authority, and the more you'll be clear about your decisions and the next steps for your life.

The word "educate" does not mean to put in, it means to pull out. It means to pull out what's already in you. It's an awareness term. The more you get an awareness of who you are, the more dangerous you become to the kingdom of darkness. If you ever want to get control of your behavior, simply get more aware.

Homework (Activation)

Also answer these two questions:

1. How do you change your beliefs about yourself? What do you normally do to impact your beliefs or do you believe that the way you think is the only way to think?

2. What are some of the greatest sources of growth that have impacted you? Has it been a conference, has it been a book or has it been a travel experience? What has impacted you that has caused you to see significant growth in your life? Write down three sources of growth. Write down three sources that you feel like will contribute to you growing in your leadership ability and your personal ability as well. Just write this in your journal. What I'm trying to do is bridge your "who" and your "do." In leadership, you have to be true to yourself regarding your mission statement and you have to be true to yourself. You may need to revisit some of those sources so that you can re-dig some wells.

Your Worldview

The indictment I have with a lot of us believers is that we sometimes pay people for things that we can google. I'm in a place in my life where I'm asking God to help me see leadership in a totally different way. I don't want to just see leadership as a boardroom, but as a person. There are still some things that need to be explored about leadership, instead of us thinking that it's about titles, positions or tasks.

The more we dig and discover our identities, the freer we will be. The more aware I am of my abilities, my capacity, my strengths, my weaknesses, my good, my bad, my sins and my mistakes, the more power I have. The Bible says that the fruit of the Spirit is love, joy, peace, patience, kindness, goodness, faithfulness, gentleness and self-control. This is why I'm trying to get you to understand that leadership isn't a task. It is about taking yourself to a destination that inspires someone else. Oftentimes, we've taught leadership as emulation. So, what we do is see what somebody else does, we get inspired by them, and then, we try to emulate them. Because of this, many people are missing their own paths. My goal in leadership is to inspire you to find your path, not find my path. Sometimes, people are afraid of lessons like this because they think that individuality will lead to dissension, but I've found that the more freedom I have, the more I'm okay being in spaces with people who aren't like me.

David said, "God, you restore my soul," but where did he say God restored his soul? The answer is: *still waters*. Why still waters? Because when you look in still waters, you'll see your reflection. Self-awareness is the beginning of soul restoration. Your soul, of course, is your mind, will and emotions. The more you are aware of your mind (the way you think), your will (the choices you make) and your emotions (the temperature produced by the way you think and the choices you've made), the more you'll have a handle on your soul; this is spiritual maturity. Spiritual maturity is having self-control of your soul. The fruit of the Spirit is a part of your soul, not just your gifting or your anointing. It's about you, the person, but you have to have self-awareness to know the person. This is important in leadership because we're struggling in a world of people who are making decisions for churches, families, corporations, our banking industry, media industry and education industry without any awareness. Their decision-making is really about what they personally think is best for other people. How can someone make a decision regarding what's best for other people without including themselves in the conversation? This is where authoritarian leadership comes from—this is when you have people who only want people to do things that only serve them, but not for the betterment of the whole. These are people who have soulish issues. This is often one of our issues in the church; we have shouted ourselves numb, we have overstimulated ourselves with church services—we have emotionally overstimulated ourselves and not had the hard conversations regarding our souls because we don't like still waters. This is because we think there's something wrong with stillness and quietness. We think there's something wrong with quiet seasons, times of contemplation, rehearsing issues and sometimes having to revisit difficulties. This is because we've been rewired to think that emotionalism is where God is, when God restores our souls in still waters.

Let's deal with the conscious and subconscious minds. Your conscious mind means the mind above, and the sub is the mind below. What we don't realize is that trauma, oppression and self-devaluation have become such a part of our subconscious that we now revere them as our normal way of thinking. Because it's now our normal way of thinking, it's become our normal way of processing behavior and making decisions. The reason that we're discussing trauma is because, if we don't deal with our subconscious, we'll never be able to reshape our leadership. When you don't deal with trauma or when you don't introduce new information to your soul (education, reading books), you will have what I call a default in leadership. Here's the truth—most people default to their emotions in leadership decisions. This is why it's very hard to move churches or organizations. When it's time to make sound decisions, people start getting into the realm of their emotions, and they start saying stuff like, "Well, I feel ..." or "I don't like." None of their decisions are made on anything that's subjective. It's all feelings-based. This is where you start to see organizations, churches and families fall apart because no one can seem to come to an agreement because their decisions and suggestions are all centered around how they feel. If I have to do or make a decision to · make you feel better, it may not always be the best decision organizationally or institutionally. The reason we have to have this conversation in innovating leadership is because we can't drive leadership forward if we don't dig backwards. We need to dig deeper. We need to start having conversations about the thoughts below our thoughts—our subconscious minds. Be transformed by the renewing of your mind. Take a moment and point to your heart. Hearts don't have brains; minds have brains. As a man thinks in his subconscious, that's the person. Have you done the hard work to reprogram how you think?

What happens if I got a virus on my computer? I would be able to log in and continue to use my computer, but when I hit a certain key or performed a certain function, that's when the virus would pop up. In leadership, the problem is most leaders operate fine until someone pushes certain buttons. A lot of people are working, living and serving at their perspective churches; they are praying, preaching and teaching—everything is fine with them until someone pushes one of their buttons. Sometimes, we simply haven't done the hard work of digging deep into our souls to pull out the past and all of those issues that are affecting us. What you continue to feed yourself is the primary way to changing what's in your subconscious mind or reinforcing what's in your subconscious mind.

Your will is the one thing that God gave you that's just like Him. Through your will, you can choose God or reject Him. This is why He says that when you pray, pray that His will be done. When you're dealing with the state of your subconscious mind and when you deal with your will and emotions, this is what makes you a very powerful leader. When you've done the hard work of healing and when you're self-aware, you won't be emotional when you're faced with hardships. I'm not minimizing your emotions. The Bible says that when someone is crying, cry with them; the Bible says that when someone is happy, rejoice with them. So, this is not me minimizing your humanity, it's about having self-control. Are your decisions controlled by your emotions? Do difficulties control your decisions? Self-control only comes through self-awareness, after all, you can't control what you don't know.

How do you acknowledge your emotions without suppressing them? The answer is in the question. Acknowledgment is key. If you're angry, acknowledge it. If you're happy, acknowledge it. Next, don't make decisions when you're in the peak of any emotional state. The Bible tells us to be angry, but sin not. You can be angry, but don't make a decision while you're angry. It's learning how to be angry, but at the height of any emotion, don't make a decision. There's a popular meme circulating that says it best; it says, "Hush until you heal."

Your subconscious mind is powered through repetition; this is why the Bible tells us to rehearse matters and this is why the Bible tells us to study because it is the will of God that you set yourself in a regiment of learning. The most powerful form of prayer is meditation. I know that we have been wired to yell at God, but it's important for us to realize that He is the King of kings and the Lord of lords. In other words, we need to be careful with the tones we use with the King of the universe. The most powerful form of prayer is meditation because it's taking God's Word from your conscious to your subconscious; this is why He said to meditate on His law both day and night. This is why, in Jewish cultures, they would take the scriptures and tie them around their arms, their hands and their heads because it was a constant reminder of the Word of God. Jewish kids, from the time they were born until they turned 12 or 13-years old didn't become citizens because they had to rehearse the law; this is a part of their rite of passage. Think about how much study and mediation they had to do to be able to become citizens. This is an art that we have lost in our faith. We've lost the time for mediation because for some odd reason, we want stimulation. Sometimes, we need to be quiet, so repetition is important. This is why our world is moving so fast; they are introducing new information to us everyday. This is also why you'll notice that I give a recap of a lot of the information I teach because I want the information to be a seed that goes in your conscious and makes its way to your subconscious.

The war between God and Satan is for your soul because whoever influences your soul influences the world. You have to know this as a leader, because whoever is the main source of influence in your life will influence your leadership decisions. If you're open and susceptible to any force, any information or any medium, anything that has an impact on your soul will directly impact the people you lead. Whoever influences the soul, influences the man. Do you want to know why Satan isn't really after your body? Because your body is the temple of the Holy Ghost. Do you want to know why Satan can't have your spirit? It's because you've already been redeemed. This is why the Holy Spirit is in your life; He is the Seal. So, Satan can't have your body, nor can he have your spirit. What does he have access to? Your soul, of course. Your soul is impacted by what you see, what you taste, what you touch, what you smell and what you hear; your soul is impacted by your senses. Sensory overload has impacted our leadership equilibrium. We are stimulated by so much stuff that many of us are no longer sound in leadership. Our equilibrium is off because of what we are constantly putting in our faces and in our ears. This includes all the stuff we're taking in—all the television shows we're watching and all the music we're listening to. This is all impacting our leadership equilibrium.

Your belief system is first of all, built by ideas. These are ideas that you've accepted by yourself. Oftentimes, these ideas have either been spoken or reinforced through experiences or behaviors. These ideas come from somewhere; they have a beginning or a root to them. At any moment, you can change what you believe about yourself. For example, at one point in my life, I had never put too much thought into my thought-life. I just accepted my thoughts, so if I had a thought or an idea about myself, I just took it at face-value. Oftentimes, we have not done the hard work of thinking about what we think about, and this is why we find ourselves manifesting and making leadership decisions while in poor states of mind. Your ideas, of course, have to come from a source. This is why we talked about the battle between God and Satan really being for your soul. Your body is God's temple; your spirit has been redeemed, so the battle is for your soul. Satan's entire goal is to have control over your soul. This is why media is important. The word "media" comes from the term "medium," which means "the space in between." What Satan is doing is using the space in between to gain influence.

When I went to teach in Haiti, I learned that they speak a different type of French than most French-speakers. So, when I was in Haiti, I needed a translator. Who was the most important person? The translator, of course. The person in between me and the people was the most important person at that moment because he had to understand and comprehend what I was saying, and then, tell the people what I was saying without changing the meaning, even if he used different words. Even though I was there to speak, he was the most important person because he had to have correct interpretation, he had to have enough words and he had to have enough understanding to take the truth that I was preaching and communicate it to the people that I was preaching to. He had to do all this in 2.5 seconds. Think about how fast he had to be. This is what leadership is; leadership is the space in between! I have to have enough language, enough experiences and enough information to communicate what God is saying to His people. If my interpretation is off, if my understanding is off or if I don't have enough words or enough education, then I'm causing people who are supposed to get the truth from God to become spiritually malnourished.

You cannot afford to have self-devaluing beliefs. You have to be aware of who you are because the world needs you. Quit perfecting church leadership. God wants us to have a broader sense of responsibility for leadership. This isn't about making you a better usher, a better intercessor, a better evangelist or a better prophet; this is about making you a better leader. Your sources are important. Let's go over a few pointers:

1. **Your precept.** You have to know what's feeding your ideas. It is the source of your ideas. This is why I told you to study, pray and meditate. You are in dominion. You are not the tail; you are the head. The Bible says that you are above only, not eventually.
2. **Your concepts.** This is where your thoughts and ideas come together.
3. **Your ideas.** This is when you have a thought, the thought comes together and forms a big picture. We

call this picture an idea.

4. **Your ideology.** This is where you form your ideas. This is where you begin to believe your thoughts. Your ideology is your believed thoughts.

5. **Your theology.** Do you want to know why this throws so many people off? Because most people think that our theology is first. This means that before you have formed your belief system about God, you have an ideology that's controlling your theology. This is why religious people exist. Religious people have an idea about God that is incorrect. The ideas that they have about God came from the wrong source. Why do people think that God is mean? The Bible says that it's the goodness of God that brings men to repentance, not the meanness of God. There are religious people who approach everything with anger, fear and resentment; they don't want to sin because they are afraid of going to hell. Their bad ideology is controlling their theology. This is important, because many of us need to have our belief systems rewired. This is why leadership is important because there are many people who's perception about God is incorrect. This is the filter by which they make decisions. For example, someone may not have a present natural father, and because their fathers were absent, they can superimpose their idea of what a father is onto God. Again, their ideology controls their theology. This is why I told you that your source is important because you have to believe the truth of scripture

over your feelings. When you become a principled leader, you become valuable. When people try to get you to respond emotionally, but you are unmoved by their antics, this is when respect is established for you as a leader. You lose respect every time you get emotional in your leadership because that's the definition of being carnal. Carnal leaders make decisions based on how they feel. Spiritual maturity is the ability to control yourself emotionally.

6. **Your philosophy.** This is your way of thinking. It is what I call your mental state. Everything, every system you feed goes through your philosophy—what you've been taught, what you've experienced, what you read, what you see—all of it is interpreted by your philosophy. Philo means love; sophy means wisdom, so philosophy is the love of wisdom. Think about the Greeks and how much they loved philosophy. For example, democracy is a Greek idea. You are living off of dead men's philosophies. This is the age of the Paulines; we know how to be in the world, but not of it. We understand the world's systems, we're intellectually educated and we're fashionable. Media is this world's god; this is why media is important for us. Media includes social media, television media, radio media, print media; think about it. The first system of libraries came through the Greeks and the Romans. So, education is literally controlled by an idea of philosophers. This is why I keep trying to tell people that philosophy is huge. We don't know

anything about philosophy in church. This is why it's dangerous to lead in church because pastors are literally dealing with uneducated people and instructing them on how to live, how to spend their money and how to raise their kids. What makes your leadership an authority is not what you say, it's the way your life serves as an example of what you've said. Your life is a measurement of your words.

7. **Your lifestyle.** If your philosophy is right or wrong, everything you hear, see or experience comes out that way. Do you know that the man sleeping under the bridge has a philosophy? But obviously, his way of thinking isn't working for him. Your beliefs are seen in your lifestyle. Your philosophy is seen in your lifestyle. The culmination of your experiences, education and beliefs is seen in your lifestyle; it's all seen in how you live your life. Jesus told us to let our lights shine before men, and Jesus came so that we can have life, and have life more abundantly. Think about the weight that scripture puts on lifestyle; He gave us everything that pertains to life and godliness. Religion wants to make us conformists. What I mean by that is, religion wants to make us hyper-moral. Many of us believe that we're right because we are on a course to eradicate sin in our lives, but sin is very easily dealt with through identity. If I deal with my identity, I simultaneously deal with my behavior. The truth of the matter is, it's all about mentality. If you change the way you think, your behavior will follow suit. This is

why we have to walk with people as a church, and we have to be patient with them. This is because people have to come to self-awareness, and the only way they'll come to self-awareness is through still waters. A lot of times we're being overly stimulated by what we call appetite. Our appetites are driven by our souls. What is your soul? It's your mind, will and emotions. Why is it that I can be watching a show on television and all of a sudden, in between that show, I'm inundated with a Big Mac commercial, a car commercial, a house commercial and a diet commercial? When I'm driving, I see billboards everywhere. Clearly, we're being inundated with all of this media or medium (in between) to control our appetites. Whoever controls your appetite can make you conform; if the media can standardize everybody's appetite, they can make everybody conform. These are the powers that you have to break free from if you're going to innovate your leadership, because you have to be okay with being the person who rejects what everyone else has accepted in an attempt to get validation, affirmation and acceptance. This is why the Bible says that he who hungers and thirsts after righteousness will be filled. In other words, he whose appetite is controlled by righteousness will be filled. This is why there are so many people in church whose appetites are controlled by mediums; the in-betweens have control of their souls.

8. **Your attitude**. This is the perspective by which you live your life. Consider the story of Joshua and Caleb. They went to the Promised Land, and the ten came back and gave their report; the scriptures said that Joshua and Caleb had a different spirit. It didn't say that they had a different Holy Ghost; what it was saying was that they had a different attitude. The ten came back and said, "They have these huge grapes over there, but they are giants! We were like grasshoppers in comparison in their eyes!" What's crazy is, they didn't ask the giants this. This was their perspective or how they saw themselves in comparison to the giants, so they called themselves grasshoppers. This is why we have to deal with the demon of self-devaluation because many of us are seeing issues in our lives that are causing us to devalue ourselves and see ourselves as nothing but grasshoppers. We're seeing the challenges and difficulties in our lives, and we're constantly saying, "That's just too big!" And we're allowing our challenges to define us. When you let the challenge define you, you're not being a leader. The one thing that made Joshua and Caleb leaders is because they surveyed the land, and they came back and encouraged the people. Do you see how powerful attitude is?

I said all of this just to deal with your worldview. Your worldview is ultra-critical in dealing with you, the leader, because if you don't have a broad worldview, your decisions will be limited. If you are close-minded, it's difficult to trust your leadership. Having a broad worldview means that you have to understand how other people live; you have to understand the dynamics of other countries and cultures. People who live for comfort or convenience will never go anywhere that requires them to be uncomfortable. When your perspective is limited to your comfort zone, it constricts your worldview and alters your ability to make sound decisions. I'll relate this to church. Some years ago, I went to Africa. While we were there, some people invited us into their homes. They were very poor people, so anything they cook for you is a delicacy and a gift. They interpret feeding you as a kind gesture and a gift. So, if someone rejects the food they've prepared, this is considered disrespectful. This is the equivalent of someone cursing us out in America. This means that I had to be okay with eating that red impala. This taught me a very critical lesson about worldviews because there are some things that we are privileged to do in America and mindsets that we have in America that wouldn't work elsewhere. Some of what we teach, preach and believe in America has not been challenged. It can't be true until it's able to be applied across the world. This is why Jesus said that He is the way, the truth and the light, because the truth of Jesus can be applied across the world. This is important in leadership because if you're trying to lead organizations and worldwide movements, you can't take what you do in America and duplicate that in Haiti. That's pride! I have to take the principal of what I'm doing here and build it based on the systems in Haiti. Many people don't understand this in leadership, so many times, they're locked in one room or way of thinking. In other words, they are limited; they can only function in one room because they don't have a broad enough worldview, a broad enough perspective or a broad enough approach to be able to change different spheres.

One of the main ways you can see the influence of a place is through their language. For example, certain neighborhoods have their own languages; certain churches have their own languages. In Haiti, the people speak Creole; this is because of the influence of another nation on their culture. We speak English in America because of Britain's influence on our culture. We speak in tongues to show Heaven's influence on our culture. So, the way that you can see the influence of a place is through their language. It's important for us to understand that if we're going to impact the world with our leadership, we have to deal with the art of language. This is why in Acts 2, the Day of Pentecost, the people spoke in tongues that other people could understand and hear. That's how the gospel went from Jerusalem to Judea to Samaria and the uttermost parts of the Earth. In Jerusalem, they spoke a language; in Judea, they spoke a language; in Samaria, they spoke a language, and the world has its own language. In your leadership, what language are you speaking? In innovating your leadership, do you have the ability to take principals and communicate them in every role or script you're put in? This is why I tell you to read books, listen to audio messages and watch videos. And don't just listen to the stuff that "feeds you" because in doing so, you can limit your mind's ability to take in new information and use what you've learned in other spaces or spheres of influence. Remember, we are called to change the world. You are called to change the world.

I believe that traditions are created wherever and whenever we don't allow or accept new ideas or new ways of thinking. In the Bible, a stronghold is nothing but a system that's shut down. A stronghold is nothing but a fortress of ideas and thoughts. I believe that we're in a dispensation where the demons we're dealing with are intellectual. This is why we're not seeing as many manifestations as we used to because we're dealing with people who are very ignorant; it's because nowadays, many people are ignorant. And because they lack access to knowledge, the way the devil moves is to make them think that deliverance is nothing but shaking and quaking all over the place. Don't get me wrong, I do believe that some people need that level of deliverance. All the same, I believe that we are living in a day where people need intellectual deliverance, and the way they get this is through truth. Jesus said in John 8:32, "And ye shall know the truth, and the truth shall make you free." We need leaders who deal with the devil today by building systems and structures that the devil can't access. We can no longer just be emotional. Have fun in church; do it all—jump around, run, dance and shout, but if we're going to impact the world, there has to be a plus to all of that. We have to innovate, we have to mature and we have to go outside the four walls of the church if we're going to impact the world. One of the reasons we're not seeing a lot of miracles *in* the church is because this is a time when God is emphasizing miracles *of* the church. He said, "These signs shall <u>follow</u> them that believe. In my name, they'll cast out devils." So, we need more miracles of the church; we need you to be the miracle. We need you to be leaders in the world and take responsibility for the difficulties that are in our world. We have to deal with these strongholds—the fortress of beliefs and thoughts that if corporately believed amongst people, have the power to create atmospheres. This is why sometimes, in church, we feel resistance; we can't seem to breakthrough. We respond by rebuking the devil; we keep giving the devil too much credit, instead of realizing that there is a collective belief system that has become an atmosphere, and it needs to be pulled down. That stronghold is pulled down through teaching. You need to embody the spirit of leadership so that wherever you are and whatever situation you find yourself in, you can become a change-agent, whether you are at home or in the workplace. People will begin to see that there is something very different about you, especially when everyone is panicking, but you haven't uttered a word.

Homework (Activation)

Take the institution of your choice: church, business or marriage. Craft three ideas on how you can expand the institution. We've used leadership to correct things, but we have not used leadership to build things. Challenge yourself with this assignment; allow yourself to feel wrong or like your ideas are not going to work. This assignment will stretch your wineskin or, better yet, your mentality. The goal is to keep you from becoming small-minded, close-minded or comfortable in leadership. Take a real scenario, and instead of identifying the problem, craft three solutions on how to expand the institution of your choice: church, business or marriage.

How to Become a Valuable Leader

Like I said in the beginning, leadership is oftentimes taught from a boardroom or positional perspective; this makes it difficult for people to see themselves as leaders. Instead, most people see leadership as a task, and because they see leadership this way, oftentimes, their decisions are based on what's in their faces as opposed to pulling deeper within themselves to discover who they truly are. If you understand who you are, this makes your leadership a million times better and a whole lot easier. This is because you'll have self-awareness; this means you wouldn't make any decisions that would inflict harm or cause difficulty in the life of someone else. Instead, you would make decisions with the intention of seeing the best in an organization or the best for a family.

We talked about innovating leadership, we talked about leadership beliefs, we talked about maturing in your personal leadership, and in this chapter, we are going to cover how to become a valuable leader. The way that you actually become a valuable person—a person who's able to hold value—is through your self-investment. What makes a diamond valuable? It's literally a piece of rock! But what makes it valuable is the amount of depth that they have to dig to get it. What makes gold valuable? The amount of depth and effort that it takes to get it! What makes oil valuable? The amount of depth that it takes to get it! Understand this—anything that is valuable has a depth to it; there's a search involved in getting to it. This is important because I have found that many of us don't search for anything anymore. The Bible even tells us to search the scriptures, for in them, you'll find eternal life. One of the reasons that some people don't find the scriptures valuable is because they don't search them. The Bible says that when you seek, you'll find; when you knock, the door opens. And oftentimes, we won't even do that for our own selves. God has hid the future of everything inside of itself. An apple has a seed, and inside of a seed is an apple. The future of your life is not ahead of you, the future of your life is inside of you. When you understand this, you will stop neglecting yourself and calling it spirituality. Neglect is not spiritual; sacrifice is spiritual. Please understand the difference. Sacrifice is what you have, but neglect is what you're refusing to manage. The Bible says to present your body as a living sacrifice, not an alive sacrifice. There are many people who are alive, but they are not living. They're alive; they're just letting life live them. In other words, they are just response-oriented. It's important for you to realize that if you are going to present your body as a living sacrifice, you must do the hard work of self-development and personal development. We don't talk about this a lot in church because we think that personal development will lead to pride or we think that self-love will lead to pride. The scriptures don't even tell us this. God said to love Him with all of your heart, your mind and your soul, and to love your neighbor as you love yourself. The key here is, you can only love your neighbor if you love yourself. Without self-investment, you won't have any love to give. The truth of the matter is, many of us have not even seen the fullness of what relationships could look like because we've come into relationships broken—we come to churches, organizations and positions unaware. And because we're unaware, we are unable to make a difference or make a dent in the lives of others.

Where you neglect yourself, you don't become valuable. I've seen many people who are just waiting on God to do something for them, when the truth of the matter is, you have to present your body as a living sacrifice, holy and acceptable to God, which is your reasonable service. The Bible isn't as complicated as many people make it; it's actually very practical.

How does one become a valuable leader? Let's look at six pointers:

1. A leader must be committed to organizational authority.
2. A valuable leader is born when leadership becomes natural and intuitive. This is when you take the information that you have in your conscious mind and you make it a part of your subconscious.
3. The more spiritually, intellectually, psychologically and emotionally stable you are, the more valuable you'll become.

4. You become valuable by taking personal initiative. You must become a leader who is proactive versus reactive.
5. Critical thinking that leads to visions being fulfilled. This is the ability to take what's in your head and put it on paper to ensure that vision is fulfilled.
6. Systems that are employed that sustain productivity and facilitate growth.

A leader who is committed to personal growth can be trusted with organizational authority. I can't trust you to make decisions that will lead and impact five-hundred people if I don't see you self-investing enough in yourself to lead you to a better place. We see people who don't read books get in boardrooms and argue with others about decisions. I've heard people on leadership teams say that they don't like to read. If you don't like to read, where are you pulling your information from? If you're a person who boasts about not liking to read, watch videos or listen to podcasts, am I supposed to take your opinion and move a church, an organization, a business or a family with it? Am I supposed to be led by your feelings? You can't be trusted with organizational authority if you're not able to show that you're doing the hard work of personal growth. You can always tell when someone self-invests because you can see it in their attitude; this is because their attitude is a combination of their education and their confidence. The reason that a lot of people have negative attitudes is because they are fear-filled. Remember, we discussed how to deal with fear. We deal with fear through education. Fear is conquered through understanding and knowledge. This allows me to have a particular attitude or spirit about myself because I understand that I have to bring my full self to any task. It's interesting to me that many people want to make decisions for organizations or families, but they don't self-invest. If you want to be a high-caliber leader, you should be self-investing everyday. Everyday, you should be reading something. Everyday, you should be taking in some level of information that sharpens your brain. You have to grow your intellect. People who are not committed to personal growth aren't normally trusted with organizational authority. There is a teaching out there that talks about people who are technicians; technicians are people who basically just perform tasks. The mentality of a technician often comes from a slavery mentality because people like this don't like to challenge themselves to research, study or dig to become better. They would rather just be told what to do, as opposed to bringing solutions to the table.

You'll become a valuable leader when leadership becomes natural and intuitive. When you discover the essence of leadership, this is when leadership now becomes second-nature—this is when you become valuable. You become valuable when leadership is now a part of you; it's natural and it's intuitive. If you understand your dominion mandate and understand that we are sons and not slaves, and you embody this and understand it, you are already in a high-level of leadership mentality. You will operate in a high leadership I.Q. when you understand that you are a son of the Most High God. A son is entitled to the inheritance and a son is not a beggar. A son operates in the same authority as the Father. When this isn't just a religious idea to you and you truly embrace it, you'll become a change-agent in the Earth. Romans 8 says that the Earth is moaning and groaning for the unveiling of the true sons of God; it says that the Earth is in chaos. It's literally like He said in Genesis —tornadoes, earthquakes, bad weather phenomena, social issues, murder, crime—all of these things are happening because sons have not stepped into their rightful places. The Earth is waiting for us to recognize our leadership authority. So, the longer we don't operate in dominion, the worse the planet gets. As the church, we have to graduate our conversations! The Earth gets worse when we don't understand our dominion. And many of us are like the Jews. We're waiting for Jesus to come back and solve the problems that we were designed to solve. Jesus even told the disciples, "Why are you all standing here in gazing? I'm going to give you someone who's better than Me; I'm going to give you the Holy Spirit." So, while many of us are praying and interceding for God to change things, God is telling us that He put us in the Earth; you're the change that the world needs to see. You're the leader who needs to involve yourself in politics and in education; you're the leader who needs to involve yourself in government, instead of sitting back and being passive in prayer. You have to actually engage culture and engage systems, not run from them.

The goal should be for the information you get to go from your conscious mind to your subconscious mind. This is so that it becomes intuitive. The reason you have to rehearse this information, continue to study it and apply it is so that it becomes a part of your natural being. So, when you're in leadership roles, when you're dealing with your family or you're dealing with society, those ideas or solutions to problems will become so intuitive that you now become a valuable solutionist. If we can get church-folks to understand this, they would stop selling their souls for a bowl of soup— they'll stop selling their souls for church titles. If you can take this information from your conscious to your subconscious mind where it becomes intuitive, then you'll become valuable to whatever you're a part of.

The more spiritually, intellectually, psychologically and emotionally stable you are, the more valuable you'll become. People can easily trust you when you are a well-rounded person. Notice, I didn't say that you had to be perfect, I said well-rounded. It means that I'm able to see your life on an ecosystem; you're making sure that you are whole: mind, body and soul. The more stable you are, the more your character is formed and the more that people see that you are engaging your intellect. Have you ever thought about this? The Bible says that the fruit of the Spirit is love, joy, peace, patience, kindness, goodness, faithfulness, gentleness and self-control. In my honest opinion, I would have thought that the fruit of the Spirit would have been gifts like prophecy or raising the dead. The Bible talked about the works of the flesh, but then it lists the fruit of the Spirit as a bunch of emotions. This has always baffled me because we, as the church, have made it all so complex. God is simply saying that you can tell when a person is mature because that person will be emotionally stable. This shows you the reality of the world that we're in. As much as you see people detaching from the church, you're also seeing more suicides and people on medication; this is because they are detaching from the spiritual place that teaches them their identities. Being spiritually mature is not about how much Bible you know; when you're spiritually mature, it's about how much Bible you do. This regulates your emotions and it makes you a mature person. What's a mature person? Someone who is able to handle difficulties! Maturity is shown in response. God said that there are going to be many people who will say that they've cast out devils and laid hands on the sick, and He's going to say, "Depart from me for I never knew you! You don't look familiar to Me!" This means that they've never grown into the full stature of Christ. So honestly, many of us should do harder work on making sure that we're more stable and we're able to respond better to change. The scripture said that if God has given you leadership ability, take the responsibility seriously. You can always tell the quality of a leader by the leader's ability to respond. This is why you're equipping yourself with new information, you're equipping yourself with knowledge and you're equipping yourself emotionally so that when it's time for you to make leadership decisions, you'll be able to respond. The Bible says we should take the responsibility seriously. It didn't say to be grim; it didn't say that we have to be mean. It said that we have to take our responsibilities seriously. This is our ability to respond. All of these things help you with your ability to respond in crisis and to respond to the necessary needs of humanity—to impact others and their lives. So, the more spiritually, psychologically, and emotionally stable you are, the more valuable you become.

Personal initiative. This is the difference between the person or the leader who is proactive versus the leader who is reactive. I think that one of the most frustrating events in leadership is having people around who offer their opinions and think that this is leadership, instead of being proactive enough to solve problems. I would rather for you to try and solve a problem, and I'm able to correct you if you're wrong, as opposed to you just giving me ideas that I have to implement to solve problems. This doesn't help me; this doesn't make you valuable to me if you're just bringing your ideas to the table, and then, I have to go and implement them. The truth is, what makes you a valuable leader is when you have personal initiative and you are able to implement solutions. If you are over a department, a family or a business, the one thing that I would hate to hear come out of your mouth is, "I'm waiting on God." That's the spirit of fear and procrastination in operation. That's a leader who isn't decisive; that's someone who doesn't want the responsibility of making decisions. Remember, we talked about sonship; we are sons. We stand in authority. We make the plans, but God orders our steps. Instead of being reactive, which is what a lot of people do. They just wait for something to happen before they respond. Those people aren't valuable people. If you want to be a valuable leader, you have to be a proactive leader. You have to take personal initiative.

A person who is a critical thinker leads to visions being fulfilled. This world has made everything easy; it's made everything convenient, but convenience doesn't change the world; critical thinking does. Critical thinking requires energy and information. If you're going to be a person who is valuable and you want to get paid top dollar, my question to you is, how critical do you think through problems? Or do you just want it over with; do you just want it done? Notice that I said critical thinking that leads to visions being fulfilled. Oftentimes, we have visions that we have never seen fulfilled; this is because of a lack of planning. I know a lot of people who have great visions, but they don't have great planning, and because they don't have great planning, they won't ever see their visions fulfilled. So, critical thinking is about your ability to put a plan together to execute the vision and make sure that it is fulfilled. This is when you become a valuable leader. Valuable people know how to put critical thinking on paper to create plans that will cause visions to be fulfilled.

If you're going to become a valuable leader, you will have to know how to build and implement systems that sustain productivity and facilitate growth. When you're the type of person who is able to build a system that ensures that things get done, nothing falls through the cracks and ensures that you're able to have measurable results, you have become a valuable leader. When you're able to sustain productivity and you're able to fulfill and facilitate growth, to change the direction of an organization or an institution, and cause things to go upward, then you become a valuable leader. People will pay you top dollar for your services or your time. Why do you go to an auto mechanic? You go to them because they solve the problem of your broke down car. This is why they are able to command a certain amount of money. They have a specific skill-set that a regular person doesn't have. Why do you go to McDonald's? Because they solve the problem of your hunger. Why do you go to the doctor? Because they solve the problem of your health. Every place that solves problems is worth top dollar. If you want to be a valuable leader, be a person who solves problems, not just identifies them.

Highlight this word: *specialization*. Specialization is having a niche area that you solve problems in; people have to turn to you because you have a specific answer for their specific problems. Can I be honest? A lot of you, because you are not self-aware, don't know your gifts. By nature of understanding your purpose, secondarily, you understand your gifts. Many people are asking the question, "What is my gift?", instead of understanding what their purpose is. When you understand your purpose, you'll understand your gift. When you understand your purpose, your gift comes with it to facilitate it. Your gift is not your purpose; this is how we've been getting confused. Many people worship their gifts, instead of realizing that their gifts are tools to help them facilitate their purposes. But when you understand your purpose, then you'll understand your gifts. When you understand your purpose and your gifts, then you'll be able to specialize in something because there are problems in the Earth that we're all called to solve; these are our areas of specialization. So, the self-development, the personal development, the self-investment, reading books, going to conferences, taking classes—all of this is to get you to dig deeper, because when you start to dig, you start to unearth. You're not going to understand everything, but you have to continue to dig. The Bible says that these treasures are hidden in earthen vessels; these are treasures that God has placed in every single one of us and your gift is where your specialization will come from. And the truth of the matter is your specialization is the place where your funding is supposed to come from. So, you will work a job until you understand your specialization, and then you strengthen your specialization before you quit your job. As you strengthen your specialization, the residuals of your specialization is able to take care of your lifestyle. This is when you can quit your job and continue to build your specialization.

Many of us say that we want to come off our jobs and do full-time ministry, but this only comes in the discovery of your specialization. You can't do full-time ministry if you're not personally developed. You have to personally grow, continually unearth what's in you and continue to make yourself valuable. Then, what happens is, your gift will begin to put you in rooms of value. The Bible says your gift will make room for you and bring you before great men. This is why you have to understand your purpose. Your purpose then teaches you your gift; you then learn to specialize in your gift and your specialization allows you to live off your residuals by doing the things that are unique and special to you.

How does one know when they're ready for ministry or when they're stable enough to do ministry? In this conversation, we have to understand the road to growth. In the church, we've been taught, what I call hyper-moralism or behavioral modification. We often think that when we're sinless, we're then qualified for leadership. We understand that when the Bible is speaking specifically about sin or sin-nature, it's talking about our positions outside of Christ, not actual behavior. So, it's showing us the realities of our "who" versus our "do" or our positions in Christ versus our positions outside of Christ. So, the Bible isn't always talking about a person's act, it's talking about a person's position. I'm trying to draw the parallel so that you'll understand that yes, you're working on your sin-nature; you're making sure that you don't have a proclivity or a mentality that drives you into a sin-nature, but all of us have our thorns in our sides. It's not the sin that disqualifies you, it's the process that you've put your life on that continues to mature you. So, the stability is about your ecosystem. How does your life run? What powers your life? What is your daily routine? Society tells us that the secret to success is found in our daily routines. What are your daily habits? Because the habits of a man are the measure of that man. Oftentimes, the way that you can tell that someone is credible is by watching their ecosystem. You can always see externally by how they live because you can hide behavior, but you can't always hide attitude. Attitude is always shown or manifesting through your words; it's shown in the weight of your words, the quality of your words and your response to problems and issues. The Bible says to watch those and to know those that labor among you. So, you are being watched; you are under surveillance. People are watching how you handle difficulties, and the truth of the matter is trauma reveals a lot about a person's growth. Oftentimes, we're rebuking trauma when trauma is a tool; it's a measuring stick of where we are emotionally. Many people don't realize that, in leadership, a lot of your job is managing crises. You cannot be afraid of crisis. When the high priests went behind the Holy of Holies, their jobs weren't attractive; they were making blood sacrifices, so I'm often perplexed by people in the church who can't handle nastiness, dirtiness, bloodiness or scandal. People who jump ship when things get nasty, bloody and dirty aren't ready for leadership; this is why there was a difference between the high priest and the Levitical order. Sometimes, people just aren't ready for the difficulties that come along with life.

We talked about people who say they're waiting on God, and

I want to bring some clarity to this. When you look in scriptures and put in the context of fasting and praying, you just don't see those things in the same context. Jesus said, "These kind come out by fasting and praying." Think about it. What "kind" did He say came out by fasting and praying? The deaf and the dumb spirit! This is why I used the word hyper-moral. Oftentimes, we're using spiritual context that doesn't apply to particular genres. How do you get a business started? You get a business started with a plan! You put a plan together, you write down your ideas, you put your ideas out there for the world to see and you educate yourself on what you need to do; this is the start and the initiation process of your reign in the business world. But nowadays, what we're doing is using spiritual language to mask our fears. When God put us in the Earth, that was His "yes." This should be super-sobering to you. When God put you in the Earth, He was finished with you. He didn't start you when He put you in the Earth. So, you have a certain amount of time from the time that you were born until the time that you die to fulfill the purpose and the plan of God for your life. You fulfill your purpose by creating systems.

Oftentimes, when we start churches, we don't build with the end in mind. So, we don't often know what our goals are. Consequently, the systems that we put in place are really just there to maintain what we have in hopes that something else will grow. I'll give you a perfect example. When is a baby is actually ready to be born? A baby is ready to be born when its systems are able to survive outside of its mother. If the systems are not able to perform on their own and the baby is born ahead of time, the baby is referred to as premature. All of your bodily systems—your cervical system, your cardiovascular system, your skeletal system— have to be able to function. What I'm saying is, in your business, ministry or whatever you are building, do you know the goal? What's your goal and how can you build a system that helps you to accomplish that goal—a system that is sustainable and not just philosophical? This means I'm able to get to my destination and I'm able to add measurable steps to get me there. And does that facilitate the ability for growth? This means, is the system flexible enough so that when things are expanding and contracting, your system doesn't kill what you're producing?

I said that the more spiritually, intellectually, psychologically and emotionally stable you are, the more valuable you'll become. I want to correct myself, but please understand what I mean when I say this. Being spiritual is an identity; it's not a behavior. This is important because, for example, I can't be Black; I am Black. So, what we have to realize is that we're a spirit put in a body and placed in the Earth. So, we are spiritual, and the reason I make that statement is to bring us to greater awareness of the fact that we actually are spiritual. We're inside a body and we possess a soul. Sometimes we use a term like "spiritual maturity" when we don't necessarily understand what it means. Spiritual maturity means to look like the reflection of Christ. He also tells us what the fruits of the Spirit are, and the fruits are all emotional fruits: love, joy, peace, patience, kindness, goodness, faithfulness and self-control. Spiritual maturity is when a person has self-control, which is spiritual control. We are in the world, but not of it. We are here to impact the world; we are here to give the world the flu—that's influence. We have to be subtle and harmless, but the church has taught us to be weird. Consequently, we are unable to have the intellectual, normal conversations about lifestyles that give us the seats of influence that causes our lives and our gifts to activate in order to make a noticeable difference in the world.

Homework (Activation)

This is probably going to be your most challenging assignment yet. Reach out to your leaders and ask them to give you some constructive criticism. The reason this is important is because the world, at large, is going to criticize you. That's a given. But you have to learn to value constructive criticism and not see it as an attack against you as an individual. Take that criticism and draw up a plan to better yourself. Submit that plan to your leaders.

The Way Up is Down

I'd like to tell you a story about an issue that we call pride. It is the enemy of greatness, even though it disguises itself as a friend of the great. This is probably a story you've heard before, but the lesson behind it will definitely help you posture yourself properly.

The story is of a major video retailer by the name of Blockbuster Video. Most of us are familiar with this retail chain. We used to go there every Friday night to find the newest horror film, comedy or movie. We'd stand in line with our rentals, excited about the night ahead of us. We'd either buy our popcorn from Blockbuster or we'd stop at a nearby store to get snacks. We would then go home or over to a friend's house to enjoy a Friday night in. So, when the retail giant went out of business, we were all caught off guard. What were we going to do now? But why the store went out of business has been a hot topic at just about every business convention. Of course, pride had its say in the company's fate.

In the year 2000, Netflix was a struggling company. They were on the brink of disaster, so co-founders and CEOs Reed Hastings and Marc Randolph set up a meeting with Blockbuster's CEO, John Antioco. They wanted to sell Netflix to Blockbuster for $50 million. Netflix was on the brink of ruins and the men hoped that Blockbuster would buy the company and turn it around. They'd heard about the brilliant mind that was John Antioco, and they believed that he had what it took to dig Netflix out of the pit it was in. They'd been requesting a meeting with Blockbuster for months and hadn't heard anything, but a mere 12 hours before the meeting, they finally heard back. They were to be in Dallas, Texas in 12 hours to pitch their ideas. The men chartered a plane and took the trip. Once they arrived, they walked into an illustrious building, filled with all of the trappings of wealth. They finally saw Mr. Antioco—a man who had once been a genius in his own right. He'd just joined the company two years prior when Blockbuster had been in a financial pit, and he'd helped turn the company around. He'd even helped the company raise $465 million the previous year through an IPO. There was no doubt in the men's minds—Mr. Antioco was a genius and he knew it. But unfortunately for Mr. Antioco, his success had gone straight to his head.

The men pitched their offer and Mr. Hastings noted how professional John Antioco had remained throughout the entire pitch. But after they were done talking about Netflix, Mr. Antioco allegedly posed a question. "The dot-com hysteria is completely overblown," he said before his general counsel, Ed Stead, butted in, telling the men that Netflix and companies like Netflix were not sustainable and would never make money. Mr. Antioco interrupted once again and inquired of their asking price. Mr. Hastings answered him.

"Fifty-million dollars," he said confidentially. It was at this moment that Mr. Hastings noticed a shift in Mr. Antioco's mood. He no longer had a stoic, professional expression on his face; instead, he almost appeared to be holding back laughter. Needless to say, Blockbuster turned down Netflix's offer and the men went home humiliated, frustrated and worried—but not defeated.

Antioco left Blockbuster in 2007 over a wage dispute. Not long after this, the company launched Total Access; this was a strategy that the company had come up with to compete with the ever-growing Netflix. Total Access was doing well; the company was starting to recover. Nevertheless, some of the investors were angry about the extra money the new service would cost them. This offer had been proposed to Antioco, but he'd been terminated before the company could reach an agreement. The new CEO, James Keyes, decided to raise the prices for online customers and turn their focus back to the store-based business. This proved to be another bad move for the company. Blockbuster filed for bankruptcy in 2010. Again, the sniper that destroyed this company was pride.

1. John Antioco refused to meet with the men for months, waiting just 12 hours before a meeting to send notice to the men that they would have to fly to Texas and be at a meeting 12 hours later.
2. Mr. Hashtings offered to sell Netflix for $50 million to Blockbuster. Mr. Antioco was too proud to see the potential of Netflix; he was still focused on a dying

market. Today, Netflix has a market cap of $125 billion.

3. James "Jim" Keyes took the company in the wrong direction. He underestimated the power of video streaming and decided to shift the focus back to store-based business.

I can't help but to think how a mind like Sam Walton would have been extremely useful had he been alive to join that meeting. In short, Blockbuster went out of business because:

1. Its CEOs were prideful.
2. They decided to go backward and not forward.

As a leader, you will find yourself having to make many decisions for the betterment or the survival of your company, organization, family or whatever it is that you are building. You will have great seasons where it will appear as if every decision you make is a genius decision. During those seasons, it will feel almost as if you're invincible. We've all been there. We've had those days, weeks or months where it seemed like everything we touched turned into gold. However, a season is just that—a season. This is why you should never allow pride to enter your heart. The scriptures tell us that pride goes before destruction and a haughty look before a fall. We can clearly see that this is true in Blockbuster's case. Pride caused the destruction of one of the greatest retail giants to have ever graced us with its presence. And of course, we could all learn a lesson from this event.

The best posture for leadership is humility. However, I believe that our definition of humility has been misunderstood and is often seen as synonymous with neglect. I've heard it said, a sign of maturity is self-celebration, however, a sign of immaturity is looking for others to celebrate you. Because leadership, to some, has the same undertones as the word "expert," those who have the privilege of holding these seats can easily slip into the mindset that they have all the answers. Society, organizations and everyday people are looking for answers to their problems, and they look to leadership for ideas and solutions. Anytime you're in a position of leadership, please know that you have been entrusted with a very valuable gift and responsibility. Don't take this lightly. It's an honor and a privilege to be trusted on stages, platforms, in boardrooms and with titles. But this privilege can easily be taken for granted if you allow pride to enter your heart.

I grew up believing that any self-focus, self-acknowledgment or self-investment would lead to pride. I thought that as long as I was doing good for others and organizations that God would take care of me. For example, I didn't eat right because I believed that, because I was doing the work of the Lord, God wouldn't allow me to get sick—or if I gave all of my money away, God would miraculously give me the money I needed. This sounds strange, but it was seriously the way I thought. I honestly thought that humility meant sacrifice. It's not a sacrifice if you don't have anything to give. Self-investment is not selfish. Selfishness is when you expect others to treat you the way you treat yourself. I can be challenged on this, but I don't believe any of us can claim to be humble until we know and understand our personal capacities. I have to know my identity, ability and capacity to it's fullest to even know where to dial it back. I have to know my scope and range to know whether I'm doing the most or not doing enough.

As a leader, it is important for you to know that the fastest way to the top is through humility. Not false humility, of course, but through true, heartfelt humility. This is when you are willing to empty yourself of everything that you are carrying in your heart. If you're scared of something, be honest about it. If you're struggling with something, tell someone who's trustworthy and wise. If you're wrestling with hatred and unforgiveness, be transparent about it. I've heard people say things like, "I just don't understand why God would bless somebody like that. She's the nastiest woman anyone could ever meet! Her attitude is always foul and she doesn't know how to treat people!" And this may be true, but consider this—is it possible that she's in the middle of a fight and the people around her are catching a few of the blows? I'm not suggesting that she should be allowed to continue mishandling people, I'm just asking if you've considered the condition of her heart. Have you ever tried to break up a physical altercation between two people, only to have one or both of the fighters accidentally punch you? In most cases, when this has happened, our adrenaline was so high that we didn't feel the pain of the punch—we felt the pressure, but not the pain. Later on, the pain may have set in, but when the punch happened, we didn't feel it. The same is true in this case. Maybe her attitude is the result of a fight that she's been in for years. Maybe she's been hurt, rejected and mishandled her entire life, and because you are within arm's reach of her, you keep catching some of the blows that were meant for the people in her past. What I've found is this—it's almost as if an unforgiving person is wearing virtual reality glasses—3D at that. While we may not see what they're swinging at, they are in a whole other world and time, experiencing something completely separate from the atmospheres they're in. And if you get too close to someone who's battling with bitterness, you will likely get punched or scratched a few times. You have to humble yourself to see her plight. She's crying out through her bad attitude; she's telling the whole world that she needs help, but if you're not humble enough, you won't hear her, and if you can't hear her, you can't reach her. If you can't reach her, you can't help her, and if you can't help her, why call yourself a leader?

The kingdom of man is designed to reflect the Kingdom of God. Your reflection is almost like a parallel world where your left eye appears to be on the right, and your right eye appears to be on the left. When you're looking into a body of water, you look down into your reflection, only to find your reflection looking up to you. As a believer, when you look at me, you're looking at yourself, and when you look at yourself, you're looking at me. What does this mean? God created us in His image and likeness; He created a reflection of Himself in us, and when we stopped reflecting His character, He knew that sin had entered our camp. He sent Adam and Eve out of the Garden of Eden, not to punish them, but He was pretty much telling them to go and humble themselves. They needed to lead themselves out of the mess they'd put themselves in, and we have to do the same. Consider this. When you see that pimp on the street, it may be possible that you are seeing yourself in another dimension. Now, this isn't a fact in the natural sense, but follow me on this. Maybe, you are seeing an issue that you have expressing itself in a body. When you see the prostitute standing on the corner, could it be that you are seeing yourself in another dimension? I'm not calling you a streetwalker, nor am I insinuating that the woman you see does not truly exist, what I am suggesting is, we all have issues. And many of our issues are under our control, but what if all of our issues could find bodies of their own to freely express themselves in? What if that desire that you've learned to suppress could step outside of your body, put on a body of its own and move into your neighborhood? I've found that the pieces and parts of our character that we hate the most tend to be highlighted in some of the people that we meet. In other words, we meet extensions of ourselves, and how we feel about ourselves will determine how we feel about those people. We've all heard some men screaming at the top of their lungs that they hate gay men, and some of them have even gone as far as to physically attack men who are struggling with homosexuality. You already know how this story ended! The men who'd so proudly and flagrantly stood up against homosexuality were struggling with that same issue. I've seen women roll their eyes at one another for no apparent reason, but because I knew them, I knew that they were simply rolling their eyes at themselves. Both women were a reflection of one another. One woman outwardly expressed what the other woman had been inwardly suppressing. This reminds me of some parents. A mother can have three daughters and hate two of them, all the while, cherishing and showering all of her love on one of them. The two other daughters represent a side to her that she doesn't like; they are outward expressions of her innermost secrets, but the other daughter is a reflection of what she loves about herself. Why am I sharing this with you? So that you can remain humble in ministry, knowing that the woman on the corner who curses you out and calls you names doesn't really dislike you. She hates herself and you appear to be an outward representation of what she's struggling with internally! If you allow her to provoke you, you'll lose a unique opportunity to reach her. To reach her, you absolutely have to humble yourself, meaning, you can't take her anger personally. I said all that to say this— leadership can be a dangerous position if your heart is not in the right position. When I stand in the pulpit at my church, I have to turn around and face the crowd. In that moment, I'm standing alone with a crowd of people facing me. My position sets me up to battle with pride. Any leader who tells you that they've never wrestled with pride is a leader who didn't resist pride when it came. In other words, they are prideful because they didn't battle with pride; instead, they embraced it. I didn't get to where I am by exalting myself; I got there by lowering myself time and time again, and I stay there by lowering myself.

As a leader, one of your greatest battles will be with pride. 1 Corinthians 8:1 tells us that knowledge puffs up, meaning, people who pursue knowledge are always pursued and often wrestled down by pride. The Bible tells us that Satan, as a roaring lion, goes about seeking whom he may devour. Can I suggest to you that he's looking for prideful, unforgiving, stubborn and religious folks? This is why the sick and shut-in list is longer than the list of attendees at religious churches. The more you learn, the more pride will pursue you because its assignment is to devour and humiliate you. To devour means to overwhelm you. When Jonah was in the belly of the whale, he had been consumed or overwhelmed by the great fish. No one could see him. No one could hear him. No one could relate to him. Have you ever been in a place where you sat next to people who couldn't seem to see, hear or understand you? We've all had those experiences, even at church. But it is during those times that we just may be in the belly of pride, trying to find our way back out. How did we get there? When our problems started mounting, we were too prideful to tell anyone out of fear that they would judge us. When our perversions kept crying out from within us, we tried to silence them by shouting the loudest and running the most laps around the church. We didn't seek wise counsel; we just thought that if we ran enough laps around the sanctuary, we could outrun it. How did pride respond? It ran with us, right past the folks that we refused to speak to because they'd offended us at some point. When we got tired, pride opened its mouth and consumed us once again; oftentimes, in the middle of one of our loudest "amens." We went home in the belly of pride, we studied the Bible in the belly of pride, we said our prayers in the belly of pride, and we tossed and turned in the belly of pride. The only way that we could get pride to spit us out was by humbling ourselves repeatedly.

Again, as a leader, you have to know that you are on pride's menu, and if you don't remain humble, you'll find yourself being the catch of the day on many occasions. This is why so many leaders battle with depression or suicidal thoughts; they have been overwhelmed by pride and religion. So, as a leader, you have to make a conscious decision to remain humble every single day. Pride can't be a part of your wardrobe. You have to model the mindset that you are advertising to others. If you remain humble and resist pride, you will open yourself up to hear more from God and to be used more by Him. This means that when you lower yourself, promotion will be inevitable. But remember, don't allow yourself to think that self-neglect, self-devaluation or self-rejection is pride. You can acknowledge yourself, your desires and your needs. There's nothing wrong with self-care; as a matter of fact, I highly recommend that you always take care of yourself before you attempt to care for others. This is why I love the safety announcements that they give on planes. They say, "Oxygen and the air pressure are always being monitored. In the event of a decompression, an oxygen mask will automatically appear in front of you. To start the flow of oxygen, pull the mask towards you. Place it firmly over your nose and mouth, secure the elastic band behind your head, and breathe normally. Although the bag does not inflate, oxygen is flowing to the mask. If you are traveling with a child or someone who requires assistance, **secure your mask on first**, and then assist the other person. Keep your mask on until a uniformed crew member advises you to remove it" (Source Air Odyssey/In Flight Passenger Announcements). In other words, don't run towards problems when you yourself have a set of problems chasing you. Deal with your own issues before you attempt to lead someone out of theirs.

The best posture for leadership is humility. This is a posture or a position that you have to maintain over the course of your life, not just your tenure in leadership. After all, remember, you are not called to do leadership, you are called to be a leader. This means that your heart posture has to change repeatedly. God will regularly update your mental software with new information, but you have to be humble enough to let Him do this, otherwise, you'll start operating in yesterday's revelation. And from there, you'll become a widow, but your spouse in the natural won't die; instead, the ideas, beliefs and concepts that you are married to—the information that you have been sourcing from will pass away because they are connected to an old, dilapidated and outdated system. And just like the widow who'd opened her home and her resources to Elijah, you'll soon discover that the old system is performance-based, meaning, you'll never be righteous under its policies. People who embrace Pharisaic theology or beliefs will tell you (if they ever have a moment of humility) that they battle with guilt and shame on a daily basis. This is because the old system is all about works, and no man can perform himself out of sin. He has to humble himself to get out.

When you turn and look at the crowd, whether you're in a pulpit, an auditorium, a classroom, a camera, a prison or in the comfort of your own home, remember that the people looking back at you need you to remain humble. They are counting on your leader-ship to take them to the next level in Christ, in ministry, in business, in their communities or in their families. Stay humble, but don't neglect or devalue yourself. Remember, the way up is down, but the way down is through pride.

I am not just creative, I am a creative. This means that everything I need to produce is locked within me. I don't have to chase success; I am success. When I embraced this truth, I became successful. As a leader, the most important dialogues that you'll have will be between you and God (in prayer) and the dialogues you have with yourself. This is why you have to break the habits of calling yourself "stupid" anytime you make a mistake. You have to learn and accept that you are royalty. I think we've all heard this before, and honestly, for most of us, this has become nothing but another self-esteem speech. But let me submit to you that it is way more than that! You have to remind yourself daily that you are royalty.

Homework (Activation)

This is the "ask a friend" challenge. Ask three of your friends if you are prideful, and if so, in what areas do they see pride manifesting in you the most. Don't do this if you're easily offended! I don't want you to ruin any relationships if you can't handle the truth or, at minimum, other people's opinions of you. And don't tell them what you think is wrong with them or where you see pride in their lives. This is about you! Don't deflect!

The Creative Leader

Over the years, we've learned to stop saying, "I am creative." Nowadays, we typically say, "I am a creative." There's a difference in the two sentences. The first sentence implies that I have a gift, but the latter implies that I am a gift. If I have a gift, it goes without saying that I can lose that gift, but if I am a gift, my giftings and callings are without repentance. In other words, nothing that I do or say can separate me from my gifts because I am the gift. In the first sentence, the word "creative" is used as an adjective, meaning, it's used to describe the subject, but in the next sentence, the word "creative" is a noun, meaning, it is the subject! Every leader is a gift to the people he or she is called or entrusted to lead. And while some gifts don't always look or sound like gifts, they often are what we need at any given moment. For example, if I buy a nine-year old boy a pair of socks for his birthday, he's probably not going to get excited about the gift. Instead, he'll open the box, lift the socks and stare at them in disgust. The sound of his mother would break the awkward silence. "Say thank you!" she would shout, hoping not to be further embarrassed by her son's reaction to his new gift. The gift didn't stop being a gift just because he didn't want it; his attitude towards the gift did not diminish its value. It simply revealed his immaturity. Of course, we all know that nine-year old boys are immature because they lack information and experience. The gift may not be what he wanted, but it may have been what he needed. The same is true for you. As a leader, you are a gift to the people you lead, even the ones who aren't mature enough to see your value. You don't stop being a gift just because someone doesn't like you or someone chose to reject you. You are a creative; you are a person who creates solutions or systems. This is what makes you a leader; this is what makes you a gift.

I am a creative. I possess the ability to create. I am a multiplier. I am a producer. I am a builder. I am a solutionist. I am a leader. Leadership isn't just about encouraging others, it's more about you encouraging yourself. The scriptures tell us that David encouraged himself in the Lord. This was the mark of his maturity; it signified that David did not rely on people to encourage him. Instead, he took the time out to encourage himself. True leaders don't depend on others to motivate, encourage or validate them. True leaders encourage themselves, even when they are in the not-so-favorable trenches of life. As I mentioned earlier, leadership is the discipline to lead yourself to a destination that inspires others to trust your steps; this allows them to find their paths to success. But what I didn't mention is this—leading yourself to a destination is not a one-time event. That's why it's called a discipline. True leadership is finding the will and the determination to pick yourself up every time life knocks you down. It means that through your perseverance, you prove to others that what they've written off as impossible is actually a possibility. Consider the story of Tyler Perry. Let's look at his timeline.

- **1992:** Mr. Perry directed, produced and starred in an Atlanta theater and failed. Only 30 people showed up for his production. He'd expected around 1,200 people to show up for that event. He'd put all of his money into this event, and this is how he ended up becoming homeless.
- **1992-1998:** Mr. Perry would do one show a year. Every year, his show would fail.
- **1998:** He was ready to give up, but decided to try one more time. This time, he succeeded.
- **2000:** Tyler premiered a play entitled, "I Can Do Bad All By Myself."
- **2001:** Tyler released "Diary of a Mad Black Woman."
- **2002:** Tyler released "Madea's Family Reunion."
- **2003:** Tyler released "Madea's Class Reunion."
- **2005:** Forbes reported that Tyler Perry sold more than $100 million in show tickets and $30 million in video sales for his stage plays.
- **2006:** Mr. Perry premiered "Madea's Family Reunion." He made $63 million with this production.
- **2006:** He wrote a book called "Don't Make a Black Woman Take Off Her Earrings." This book earned him two awards.
- **2007:** He premiered the hit movie "Daddy's Little Girls."
- **2008:** Released "Why Did I Get Married?"
- **2008:** Mr. Perry premiered "The Family that Preys."

- **2009:** Released "Madea Goes to Jail."
- **2010:** Tyler released a sequel to "Why Did I Get Married?" entitled, "Why Did I Get Married Too?"
- **2012**: Released and starred in "Good Deeds."
- **2019:** Tyler Perry opened his own film studio.

Of course, this is not a full timeline of his career. The truth is, Mr. Perry has been and remains a very busy man. Get this— everybody has his or her own world. I'm not talking about a planet, I'm talking about a system, howbeit, we can liken it to a planet for the sake of this presentation. And everybody is lord over his or her own world; this is why Jesus is King of kings and Lord of lords. In my world, what I've written off as impossible has become impossible to me because I've created the laws of that world. In your world, there are a few things that you've written off as impossible, so they may never come to pass for you; that is, unless you change your mind. But for Tyler Perry, what you and I wrote off as impossible, he decided was a possibility, even when he was homeless. When all of our worlds connect, they create the systems of this world. So, if we would have said to Tyler back in the day that he could not accomplish the feats that he has accomplished, we would have served as resistance or warfare in his world. This is why we have to encourage one another; this is why we should never superimpose our negative views or beliefs on others. This is also why we need to surround ourselves with positive people. We need people who are quick to encourage and edify others. Again, through your leadership, you prove to others that what they've written off as impossible is actually a possibility. This is exactly what Mr. Perry did. What he accomplished falls within the realm of impossibilities for most of us, but he proved that they are possibilities for all of us. Let's define the word "impossible."

- unable to exist, happen, or be achieved; not possible (Source: Cambridge Dictionary)

Let's get one thing straight. The word "impossible" has the same meaning, but is interpreted differently by most people, depending on what side of the Leaders' Spectrum they fall on. At some point, you were an impossibility, your car was an impossibility and airplanes were an impossibility, but somehow, the mold was broken and you came into existence, along with every other impossibility. Today, the Great Pyramids are still a great mystery; they still appear to be an impossibility; people are still trying to figure out how the Egyptians pulled off such an amazing feat! The point is, the word "impossible" is a subjective word. Hear me—leaders come on levels. Some leaders take what others have created and enhance them. Other leaders create things from scratch. They may use the scientific research that has been gathered over the years to tell them if their crazy ideas are plausible, but the most renown and respected leaders are the ones who make the impossible possible! Is it possible to create a train that flies? Yes, it is—someone has already coined the idea and put together a blueprint, however, it still appears to be an impossibility. This is because we don't all understand aerodynamics. Think of your wildest imagination and ask yourself, "Is it possible?"

I'm not talking about spiritual things; we know that God can do anything but lie—I'm talking about creating something material that could be used in the Earth. We've all come across a group of Black males who've blamed their misfortunes on "the man." We've listened intently as they strung together some elaborate words, gave us a few history lessons and repeatedly pointed at their brains every time they mentioned the power of knowledge. We've monitored their overly animated hands, and did our best to avoid getting our eyes plucked out. This blame-game is the reason there are so many educated Black men sitting in prison cells. They tried to "stick it to the man" and ended up getting stuck in prison, where they proceeded to "drop knowledge" on anyone who couldn't figure out a good enough excuse to escape their long speeches. This isn't to make fun of them, of course. What I'm saying is, knowledge, when paired with blame, is called religion. Howbeit, Tyler Perry, like so many other African men and women, chose a different path. They chose the barely beaten path of accountability. This isn't to say that we haven't been oppressed as a race; this is to say that no one has the power to hold us back if we're determined enough to go forward. Non-leaders string together excuses, but true leaders are too zealous (stubborn) to quit. Again, true leadership is not a one-time event; true discipline is the result of repetition.

As a creative and a leader, you can't be afraid of going against the grain of what society calls normal. Martin Luther King, Jr. went up against social norms, Susan B. Anthony went up against social norms and Nelson Mandela went up against societal norms. Leaders who are afraid of confrontation are rarely remembered or celebrated; we remember these three amazing souls because they left their imprints on our world as a whole. They made so much noise that we can still hear their voices echoing in our culture today, even though they have all passed on. They didn't allow the threats or the violence around them to drown out the noise of their assignments. They didn't fancy fitting in over standing out. I mentioned this because this is one of the most pronounced issues you'll find in leadership today. Most leaders want the benefits of both worlds—they want to be normal and fit in; then again, they want to be leaders. Being a leader and fitting in doesn't go in the same sentence; these two worlds cancel one another out. I've found that the reason most leaders want to fit in is because they don't want to deal with the noise that people make anytime they realize that change is on the horizon. I compare this to taking keys from a baby that's awake versus waiting for the child to fall asleep to quietly slide the keys from its tiny grip. If a child is holding a set of my keys and I need those keys, that baby is going to cry. I'm not being insensitive—I'll be gentle when I take them away from him; what I'm saying is, we take things from children early so that we can prepare them for the world and the IRS. Crying won't hurt the child; it only teaches the infant that he cannot control anyone by being emotional. This is what we, as leaders, do to the world. We take away beliefs and systems that they don't need or can't use, and we ignore the yells, the profanities and the threats of violence so that we can implement something better. We can't just wait for them to be distracted and try to slide change into their lives. Have you ever tried to take your keys from a sleeping baby? If you have, chances are, the baby woke up and started screaming. The same is true for the world. When people are comfortable with systems and programs, they'll whine and complain anytime those systems and programs are brought under review. They curse and fight when someone tries to make changes to those systems. As leaders, you have to be willing and able to count the costs associated with your assignment, otherwise, you'll conform. You won't make any changes, but instead, you'll go down in history as a nobody. Nobodies give the people what they want, which is just a polished version of what they already have. I don't believe that any of us were created to be forgotten. Howbeit, if you want to be remembered, you have to be willing to do the hard work of building programs, systems, organizations and institutions—yes, even if what you're building goes against societal norms. It goes without saying, I'm not telling you to build anything perverse, blasphemous or offensive; I'm simply saying that if some man says that the Earth is flat, and the people at large accepts this theory, it's okay for you to prove that the Earth is round.

You are a leader and you are a creative. One of your assignments is to create solutions, and remember, not all problems look like problems. A lot of leaders only tackle the issues that people complain about, but a good leader solves problems before they come into the realm of reality. For example, if I decided to manufacture airplanes, I would draw up a blueprint, and then, I'd ask myself the following questions:

1. How do I create something that's different from every other plane on the market?
2. My plane will be similar to the Boeing 737. How many times has that particular brand of planes crashed, and for what reason? What can I do to my plane to ensure that my passengers don't suffer the same fate?
3. How do I create more legroom without minimizing the amount of passengers my plane can carry?
4. How do I give my Economy class passengers a First Class experience, while giving the people in First Class a royal experience?
5. What are some effective security measures that we can implement?

As you can see, some of the questions are centered around the problems that other air carriers have, but others are centered around creating solutions that are not necessarily centered around problems. Solutions to problems that are not really problems are called luxuries. So, if I give my Economy class passengers a First Class experience, what I've done is spoiled them. Doing this would make it harder for them to fly with other airlines. This would raise their standards, all the while, helping them to remain within their budgets. Of course, I'd probably charge a little more than most, but not much. What I've done is called creative thinking; this is me exercising my ingenuity. As a leader, I didn't create a plane and wait for the naysayers to complain about the plane. Instead, I created a plane that's safe, luxurious and affordable. Do you see failure in my future? Of course not! Why? Because I answered questions that had never been asked or, at minimum, posed to me. I took the lead and I proved to myself and others why I am the leader. Guess what? This is what I do with my church and everything I create. I see myself as a pilot, but I don't sit around and wait for problems to materialize. I'm always looking at ways to make the members' experience a lot better; I'm always looking at ways to expand and improve what I have. This is good stewardship. How you steward what God has given you will determine if He will dare to trust you with more. As a solutionist, you should never wait for naysayers to say something. Fix what they would complain about before they say something, if at all possible!

Let's Go to Church

Maybe you haven't created anything yet. You know that you are talented deep down inside, but you've never tapped into that part of yourself or you've never fully tapped into that part of yourself. For this reason, you are somewhat insecure. To rectify this, you have to remember that you are the gift; if you keep placing emphasis on your creative abilities, you'll keep discounting yourself, however, if you allow yourself to believe that you are the gift, you'll learn to be just that—a gift. In other words, if you're in a church, serve. And don't just serve, do it in excellence. Utilize your creativity to propel the church forward. This isn't just about your abilities, it's also about your availability. You see, there are a lot of creatives in churches who won't sacrifice their time, especially if what they are required to do doesn't immediately benefit them. There are people in churches who are masters at graphic design, but they would never create even a flyer for their churches unless their faces are on those flyers or unless the church pays them for their work. In other words, they are self-centered; they see the small picture (themselves) but not the big picture (the church as a whole, the body of Christ). I'm not suggesting that folks should just allow themselves to be taken advantage of, but at the same time, I personally don't think your home church could use or take advantage of you. Why not? Because just like your tithes belong to your local assembly, your gifts were given to you to not just use in the marketplace, but in your local assembly. If you must get paid for your work, try not to empty your church's treasury, after all, you are getting fed there. Now, if your church needs a lot of your time, and this is taking away from your ability to make a living, it's okay to talk business. But if your church isn't hurting your business, and you can afford to spare some time and share your creative abilities with your local assembly, please do so without taking them to the bank. It's hard to teach this because so many people have been used and taken advantage of outside of the church, so by the time they come into the sanctuary, they are suspicious of everyone. Consequently, messages like this don't carry over well with them. Instead, they filter everything through their hurt and their experiences. As a leader, you can't run around thinking that everybody is trying to take advantage of you. Suspicious leaders always end up sabotaging their relationships and shutting doors in their own faces because they have not taken the time to deal with their past hurts. Sure, there are some people who will see your gifts and want to access them freely, but your job isn't to guard your gift, it's to guard your heart. You see, when you try to guard your gift, you essentially forget that you are the gift and you'll end up getting hurt because you'll try so hard to guard your hands that you'll forget to guard your heart. I've seen people do this; they've gotten offended because they felt used, and because of this, they found some disgruntled church member or ex-member to express their grievances to. That member or ex-member gave them what they wanted—the confirmation they needed to break away from their local assemblies. They then left the church screaming, "church hurt," simply because they neglected to guard their hearts. To guard your heart means to monitor what goes into your ears and your eyes. If you fail to do this, you will use your creative abilities everywhere except your local church. Eventually, someone who is a gift just like you are who has the same talents will submit their gifts; they'll go through every season of feeling stretched, used and unloved, but eventually, they'll mature. When they do, their gifts will open doors for them and bring them before great men. What are their gifts? Is it their creative abilities? No! I think that we, as the church, have largely misunderstood this scripture. Their gifts are not their talents; it's the people who they served! Need proof?! Ephesians 4:8-14 says, "Wherefore he saith, When he ascended up on high, he led captivity captive, **and gave gifts unto men.** (Now that he ascended, what is it but that he also descended first into the lower parts of the earth? He that descended is the same also that ascended up far above all heavens, that he might fill all things.) **And he gave** some, **apostles; and some, prophets; and some, evangelists; and some, pastors and teachers**; for the perfecting of the saints, for the work of the ministry, for the edifying of the body of Christ: Till we all come in the unity of the faith, and of the knowledge of the Son of God, unto a perfect man, unto the measure of the stature of the fullness of Christ: That we henceforth be no more children, tossed to and fro, and carried about with every wind of doctrine, by the sleight of men, and cunning craftiness, whereby they lie in wait to deceive."

The gifts are not your creative abilities; it's the leaders who God places in your life! We've been preaching this thing wrong the whole time! That's why there are so many creatives out there who have amazing creative abilities, but no platforms. They reduce their talents by refusing to submit them, only choosing to exchange their abilities for money. And this is why they never go before great men; they robbed the gifts that were in their lives because they were too busy worrying about somebody using them! But the gifts who serve with joy find themselves in rooms that they never thought they'd enter. Why? Because their gifts (their pastors, evangelists, teachers, prophets or apostles) made room for them! Again, I'm not saying that you shouldn't charge for your services; what I am saying is, give as much as you can afford to give, but once you go beyond that, then talk business. There is a season of leadership where you are hidden, but your talents are on full display.

During this time, you can't pull back just because you don't feel like you're getting the recognition you deserve. Instead, you press forward until every ounce of ambition dies; you press forward until feeling ignored, underappreciated or invisible is no longer a problem for you. All of these feelings occur during the infancy stage, but as you grow, your eyes will open to see the big picture.

Let's Go to Work
If you're working for someone, use your creativity to help move the company forward. In other words, be a valuable asset or a valuable leader everywhere you go, even when you don't have the titles, functions or the authority of a leader in your organization.

Let's say, for example, that you go to work and notice a poorly designed flyer plastered to the bulletin board. You're a graphic designer, so you shake your head at how cheap your employers are. You have two choices in that moment. You can go home (when your shift is over) and create an excellent flyer to replace the one on the bulletin board or you can tell everyone with a working set of ears how terrible the posted flyer is. The most you'll get if you do this is someone will say, "They should have hired you." This is just their way of ending the conversation and flattering you at the same time. But if you replace the flyer, you present yourself as the gift you are. Get this—your company may start hiring you to create their graphics. Or there is the possibility that they'll ask you to create them freely. If this happens, you can choose to say yes or no. Personally, I'd do the work because that little act of kindness could open some major doors for you in the organization. As a creative, it is important for you to always look at the long term benefits versus the short-term inconvenience. Of course, how you use your creative abilities is one hundred percent up to you. These are just suggestions.

Maybe, you are not a graphic designer; maybe, your strengths are punctuality and loyalty. Believe it or not, these attributes make you a very valuable leader. Truth be told, these attributes make you far more valuable than a person with twelve talents who cannot be relied on. Every organization, institution or establishment wants to have people that they can rely on; these people are often trusted into rooms that others are not allowed in. They are gifts to any organization. But again, maybe your strengths are loyalty and punctuality. You don't make excuses, nor do you complain. Instead, you come to work on time, show up for every meeting and you encourage others to do the same. What you're doing is still leading, even if you don't have a title or any authority in your organization. By you showing up at the meetings on time, you not only create a standard, but you also make it hard for other employees to show up whenever it's convenient for them. You are a gift; use your creative abilities to pull your company forward; yes, even if you are not a fan of the people who are in power. One of the most tried and effective ways to elevate in any organization is by not being emotional or vengeful. You simply forgive and continue to be the gift that you are! Sure, it's not easy to work under someone who has a heavy hand or a heavy heart, but as a leader and a gift, you have to remember to never take professional issues personally. In other words, guard your heart. Buy your boss a gift. Smile at him or her everyday. Greet your boss. Compliment your boss. Again, what you're doing is leading. You're leading your boss out of his or her incessant need to belittle, berate or micromanage you. You're leading in love, and this isn't an easy task; that's why it was cut out for leaders only. Leadership is not dictatorship; it's twenty percent talk and eighty percent demonstration.

Let's Get to You

What are you struggling with in your own personal life? Is it unforgiveness? Is it lust? Are you someone who runs every time the going gets tough? What is your Achilles heel? Let's go back to the examples I shared earlier. First, let's deal with the mold or the clay mask. I used the example of a woman being in a museum, where she sees a mask that hasn't fully dried yet. She touches the mask before it dries, causing her fingerprint to embed itself within the mask. When the mask hardens, her fingerprint is the equivalent of trauma. It's one of her imperfections. As a leader, you are covered with fingerprints—some of them are points of trauma, while others are the fingerprints of the people who've made a positive impact on your life. Listen to me—you've got to deal with them. Remember, you are creating a mold that someone else will someday use. Whatever issues you don't deal with, you'll leave that same impression on the lives of everyone you touch. This is why there are so many individuals, organizations and institutions out there that can't seem to grow. Every time people walk through their doors, they end up getting traumatized. If you're going to be trusted with the hearts and minds of many, you will have to deal with your traumas. Stop writing them off as if they don't exist and just confront them. Trauma is like a roaring lion; it has claws and teeth. It tears through our souls without mercy. It devours our peace and our relationships day after day. And this is why we have to confront it. This is why we have to kill it. We then take the jawbone from it and use it to overcome every donkey or stubborn spirit that dares to rise up in our lives. Of course, Samson took the jawbone of a donkey, but we have to take the jawbone of whatever Goliath we find ourselves wrestling with. If trauma is your giant, overcome it and take away its jawbone. This takes away its ability to continue speaking in your life. The point is, you have to get healed. This isn't an option. If you're going to successfully lead anyone to victory, you have to first come out of your defeated place and drag yourself into your seat of authority. Your seat of authority is found in your healed place. If you make a throne for yourself in your pain, you will soon learn that your throne is the equivalent of what we refer to in America as a porcelain throne. It's a toilet. It's just a place for you to air out all of your grievances in a way that causes others to avoid you. Heal!

Next, I compared you to a building. Every building has a foundation, every building has walls and every building has a roof. Your foundation is whatever it is that you are building your life on or whatever it is that you're building your case on; it's the legality behind your existence. Are you building on the Word of God? If so, that's your legal grounding. Are you building on your pain? If so, that's your legal grounding. Every brick put into your structure represents an event; it's a fact or your perception of an event. It's been sealed together by your memories of each event and your takeaways from each event. If you have any bad bricks in the building, you are insecure. Now, let me stop for a moment and say that not every loud, overly confident person is secure. Insecurity can manifest itself in several ways. With some people, it manifests itself as pride, confidence and boldness. With others, it manifests itself as timidity, lack of confidence and fear. But the root behind all insecurity is fear. Faith stabilizes a structure, but fear destabilizes it. The roof is another foundation. It holds the issues beneath it together and covers you, disallowing any new information to come in. This is pride. The walls are the beliefs and the people you use to surround yourself with. These are what and who keep you from escaping the structure that you built while traumatized. But you have to abandon that building. You can't keep living in it, waiting for God or some human to come along and create a better place for you. Jesus already gave you what you needed; you can now live and rest in Him. You can now build on solid ground, and you can be built up with good memories. The old building will keep standing, but you can't keep living in it if you want to be an effective and impactful leader. It becomes nothing more than a museum that you can take people by to show them the distance between where you are today and where you lived at one point in your life. You shouldn't be still living in the ruins of your past life.

Let's Get to Others

Once you've abandoned the waste places that you once called home, your next assignment is to lead others. Your story will help them, of course, but don't try to lead people with your pain. You can show people your scars, but don't forget to cover them back up and show the people your victories. Otherwise, they'll focus on you and your scars, rather than the big picture. This is how gangs are created. Some broken and hardened soul shows a few guys his bullet wounds to gain their admiration and to strike fear in their hearts. But this is not how we lead. I show my scars when I need to show them. This is wisdom. I show my victories, and when someone comes along who needs to see my scars, I show them. Leaders who build organizations and institutions on their pain create gangs. That's why the people around them are goons. That's why some of their followers are willing to serve life sentences trying to protect their names. This isn't leadership; it's gang activity. It's criminal behavior. And sadly enough, we do see leaders like this rise up even in the church. They create networks and secret societies that only serve them, not the people who follow them. These leaders live in fear; they're insecure because they haven't dealt with their hurts or their histories. Hear me on this—no true leader needs goons. We help broken people get healed; we don't turn them into a mob of angry pit bulls, and use them to protect us. This is the mark of a coward. Please note that goonish people idolize their leaders; this is what makes their relationships so dangerous. If you surround yourself with broken people, and you use their brokenness for your benefit, it'll only be a matter of time before they turn on you. It's a rule of nature.

You are designed to help others. You have to lead yourself to a destination and then show others how to do the same. Sure, people are going to come along and offer to do some goon-work for you because this was how they found their value in the world. They didn't know how valuable they truly were, so they advertised themselves to the world as crazy. They did crazy things, served time in prison, refused to snitch when questioned and they went above and beyond to prove their loyalty. They didn't do this because they were loyal; they did it because they were broken. They were love-starved. Their craziness had once been valuable to them; it's all that they have or all that they think they have, so when they come along and offer it to you, don't embrace it. Embrace the person that the world rejected. Embrace the real person underneath the labels. This is how you pull him out. This is how you pull her out. This is how you pull them out. They are still love-starved. They're hoping that if they offer what they believe to be their strengths to you that you'll eventually love and appreciate them. It's only a matter of time before they realize that you were just another person who used them. You may be the person who gets them to their breaking point because they thought that there was some good left in the world, and you were the evidence of that. If you take this away, you take away all of their hope. A man who has lost all of his hope is a very dangerous man. Don't flash your scars before them; show them your victories. This is what they need to see. Scars, for broken people, are like tattoos. They only admire them. Love them, lead them and help them grow into the pillars they were designed to be.

Your Leadership Unlocked

I used to think that I was building a structure; I was building a church. Of course, I wanted that church to expand, but my vision, while big, was nowhere near what God had planned. As you build, your eyes (vision) will get bigger and sometimes, it will feel like your dreams are too big for you. The old folks used to say, "Your eyes are bigger than your stomach!" This simply meant that you'd put too much food on your plate and you were not going to be able to eat it all. Sometimes, we surprised them. What did we do? We ate it all and went back for more. Before long, our stomachs were bigger than our eyes. And this is when we realized that we needed to do something; we needed to implement exercise into our diets. I love going to the gym nowadays, and I've learned a few things about myself since I started my new lifestyle. First off, you'll notice that I don't call it a journey; a journey implies that there is a destination, and once we've arrived at that destination, we can stop moving. When it comes to building your body, you can never quit, even when you have the perfect body. This is because you're building more than muscle, you're also building your confidence, your stamina and you're building up the confidence of the people who watch you from near or afar. I say that to say this— leadership is not about stopping; it's about becoming the best version of yourself and teaching others to do the same.

Again, I used to think I was building a structure. Eventually, as the dust cleared, I realized that I was building a city or an empire. In the biblical days, a city was the equivalent of a kingdom. I had to stop limiting myself because of the expectations of religious folks; I had to give myself permission to see the big picture, and then, I had to see me in the picture. And like you, that picture was exciting, but scary at the same time. If you're not intimidated by your vision, it's way too small! But just like I'm building my body, I'm also building a legacy.

To build a structure, you have to fully unlock your potential. I've found that most people are terrified of their own potential. Most people can only handle snippets of God's plans for them. This is because the big picture doesn't include some of the folks that we want it to include. I personally believe that if we were able to see a full picture of God's plans for us, most of us would tremble with awe and fear. We'd be afraid of living the lives that we saw in our visions because that new place would look so foreign to us. At the same time, we'd be excited about what is to come. But because of the love that we have for some of the people and systems currently in our lives, we'd probably sabotage our futures trying to change the endings; we'd try to find some type of way to keep some of the relationships we have from expiring. I'm in no way suggesting that you won't recognize anyone around you. I believe that a select group of people will come with you, go before you or come because of you. If we saw the big picture, we'd spend excessive amounts of time trying to convince some of the folks around us to change. We'd panic and plead with them to change. And this is why our futures are so blurry to us. We often see chapters and verses, but we don't see the entire picture. If we saw it, we'd be trying to pencil the folks in that God has erased.

You have potential, but potential just means that you have the ability to be potent; you have the ability to be powerful. Not everyone who has potential maximizes their potential. The average human being buries his or her potential in favor of being comfortable. You see, when you start unlocking your leadership potential, you'll find that most of your comfort zones will slowly or sometimes suddenly become waste places. They will become ghost towns, and before long, you won't have many comfort zones to hide yourself in. When you become comfortable being uncomfortable, you are ready to unlock your creativity—you are ready to be the leader you were designed to be. Some people are slaves of comfort. We've all served time in our comfort zones; some people have decided to give themselves life sentences with no possibility of parole or growth. They've locked themselves in their comfort zones and they refuse to come out. As a matter of fact, if you try to pull them out, they will reject you as a leader. Most leaders who are rejected often by their students are change-agents. They keep pulling people out of their places of comfort; sometimes, prematurely. This is why you have to be sensitive to movements and moments. You have to know when to pull, when to push, when to be still and when to let go. You also have to know when to snatch folks because some people aren't coming out unless somebody snatches them. But again, you have to be sensitive to these moments. You can't just go by your feelings. An emotional leader is an unstable one. I'm not saying that you can't have emotions; what I'm saying is that if you are going to be a change-agent, you can't be controlled by your emotions and you should never use your emotions to control others.

Your full leadership potential is locked behind your yes. When you start seeing the full vision, you can't shrink in fear and then hide behind religion. Sometimes, you have to see the picture, numb yourself and just shout "yes." It won't make sense to you in the beginning, but eventually you'll come to appreciate the fact that you are one of the few people who were bold enough or crazy enough to say yes. Most people see a snippet of the vision and shrivel up. They let fear control their destinies, and consequently, they allow their fear to control the destinies of others. This is why you can't just follow anybody. You need to follow change-agents; you need to follow doers. These are your producers. Many people are out there following folks with big mouths but no results. These are the people who talk a good game, but the minute they are tossed into the lions' dens, they try to make a deal with the lions, rather than using their creative abilities to give the lions an ultimatum. You tell the lion, "I'm going to give you two choices—either I can kill you and take your jawbone; that is your voice or you can shut your mouth."

I am a timeline in the making and so are you. Look at your creative abilities, and then, put them to use. Don't take too much time off from being creative because you are a creative. In other words, you'll get to know you more through your creativity. Your creativity may express itself in graphic design, taming animals, administratively or through your punctuality. It amazes me that some people still say that they don't know what their talents are when they are sitting right there in their faces. Your creative ability may express itself through your loyalty. In a world of disloyal, unstable people, you lead people through your loyalty. There are people in spaces right now who are still there because they are patterning themselves after the loyal people in those spaces. They've never been taught to be loyal; they've never experienced what it was like to sit still, especially when they were in pain. They look at others to see how they should respond. They know how they would've responded in the past, but they've chosen to be the best versions of themselves possible. They simply don't know how to commit to anyone or anything, but if your strength is loyalty, please note that your gift is perseverance. That's all loyalty is. It's refusing to give up even when it makes sense to do so. When people see your gift in action, it inspires them to be loyal; it inspires them to persevere. Then again, you may have the gift of gab. This is a gift that not everyone appreciates, but it is a gift nonetheless. You are the gift. You're a gab-gift, not a gag gift. Meaning, there are some people out there who need to hear what you have to say. You are a teacher; you build line upon line and precept upon precept. You just need a leader to examine you and tell you when to push the off button from time to time; that is, until you learn when to turn it off on your own. These are all talents. Sometimes, we misuse them or we use them in spaces when they are not appreciated, but if you don't bury them, you'll eventually unlock their potential.

Your ability to create coupled with your willingness to create is what makes you a creative. Your willingness to sacrifice the time, effort and money it takes to produce a product, a service, an organization, an institution or a solution is what makes you a leader. This world is full of problems, and I dare to say this—any person who makes it a point to run towards problems that are running towards them is a problem-solver or a solutionist. A solutionist who learns to overcome a certain area of problems *in excellence* is what we call an expert. A solutionist who teaches others how to chase and overcome their own problems is an example. The world is full of problems; the world is full of consumers. This is why one percent of income earners own more than half of the world's wealth, while 90 percent own 71 percent of the world's debt. How do we move from being a consumer to a producer? By talking less and doing more. Consumers are complainers; they are masters of lip service. Let's look at the Leaders' Spectrum one more time.

Consumers/ Complainers 30%	Spectators/ Procrastinators 60%	Producers/ Solutionists 100%

A large number of leaders are stuck somewhere around 40 percent. The majority of leaders are stuck in the middle of the spectrum; this is the planning stage. This is when we have a ton of ideas, but little to no execution of those ideas. To move across this spectrum, you have to understand that there is going to be opposition. You will want to quit! And the more you ascend to the producers' side of the spectrum, the more betrayal you'll experience. Some people even say it's lonely at the top, and while this can be and often is true, it's really just a matter of perspective. If I'm at the top, my need for validation or human interaction significantly decreases but does not dissipate. Instead, I learn to value qualities like loyalty, patience, kindness and peace all the more. This is because the move towards the top of the spectrum can be noisy, and for some people, it can be bloody. Of course, I'm not talking about bloody as in somebody dying, I'm talking about bloody, meaning, they have hurt themselves quite a bit along the way and they've been hurt quite a bit along the way. If you look at many of the leaders I mentioned in this book, you'll find that they have seen their fair share of hurt, betrayal, rejection and sorrow. But unlike the average person, they decided to persevere. Perseverance is a personal choice. Most people don't see the value in forgiving others or persevering through the storms of life; this is why they choose to remain angry at the folks who hurt them. To move along the Leaders' Spectrum, you have to be willing to forgive, to heal and to keep pressing! You can't be wound-focused! Remember, this is what gang members do! They point to and platform their bullet wounds in an attempt to make themselves relevant and feared. But this isn't what we do! Your wounds are not your tickets to greatness; they are your stretch marks! Again, a large number of leaders are stuck in the middle; they are caught up in the planning stages. I've found that most people in the planning stages get stuck because they keep making plans, but they rarely execute. They then begin to manipulate themselves by saying things like, "I was going to start on this business, but God told me to do the book first," or vice versa. They keep this up year after year, always using God as a cop-out for their laziness and their fear. I love Nike's slogan; it says, "Just do it!" Listen, it is better to do the work and fail; this way, you can learn what you've done wrong than it is to keep sitting on your talents like a mother hen sits on her eggs. If those eggs hatch and she kept sitting on them, she'd suffocate the babies or they'd starve to death. Are your talents hungry or are you too busy feeding your fears with your excuses? If you keep feeding fear, it keeps getting bigger. If you keep starving your creative abilities, they keep getting smaller. It is no wonder that fear keeps consuming your plans! At some point, we have to come out of the planning phase; we have to take our pencils off the paper and execute what we've written! We can't keep writing and planning; this is fear and procrastination in full effect! We have to get past these two if we are going to become impactful, effective and valuable leaders. Below are 12 steps to maximizing your leadership potential:

1. **Leadership + creativity = power:** In other words, you have to produce! And the first thing you have to produce is a disciplined leader within yourself. You have to lead yourself to the destination that you plan to lead others to. This requires your creativity. Remember, another word for creativity is strategy. In other words, you have to develop a series of strategies to pull yourself out of the pits of mediocrity that you've fallen into, and then, use those strategies to help pull others out. This is what makes you potent; this is what makes you powerful! Don't overthink it; just produce. Electricity, which we know to be power, is produced by the kinetic energy of flowing water and wind. Flowing water is water that's moving; water that does not move is infested with bacteria and stagnant! Wind represents the opinions of others. This is what should push you forwards, not backwards. You have to have a strategy in order to move, especially when you're having to get around the opinions, rumors and lies that people are going to throw at you. But this is what produces power in your life.

2. **Change your thought life:** You do this by constantly introducing your mind to new information. This is why leaders are called gifts. They bring you new

information. Study, read books and go to conferences. Don't just sit in your home, thinking that someone, somewhere is going to somehow discover you and open up doors for you. That's not how this works! You have to be willing to come outside of your comfort zone in order for your mindset to be challenged and confronted—this is the not-so-pleasant side of becoming an impactful leader. Honestly, it does get easier, then it gets better, and before long, you'll start to enjoy having your beliefs examined and challenged. Your thought-life controls every aspect of your existence; this is why it is necessary to change it. People who refuse to change their minds, quite honestly, become rigid and religious. They also don't age well. Get out of your comfort zone and cram your head with knowledge! This is why so many people read one book, and suddenly, they buy whole libraries of books; they essentially become book nerds because they love how knowledge has impacted their lives. They love going into environments filled with thinkers who challenge the way that they think. But the people who fear knowledge, correction or being stretched spend their lives surrounded by people like themselves. They spend their lives in small spaces, surrounded by small-minded folks with big mouths and no vision. Change the way you think! Do it one book at a time, one conference at a time, one convention at a time and one conversation at a time. Whatever you do, don't settle with what you know—

learn!

3. **Build your leadership profile:** I'm not talking about a profile online! I'm talking about the mold that others will someday measure themselves by. You do this by developing your character, overcoming your giants and submitting yourself to others for examination! Remember, your mindset isn't just being molded by the information that you willingly take in, it's also be challenged and pressed by your experiences. If you have a bad experience, go read a book about it. Get counseling if you need it. Talk to your leaders about it if you don't understand what you've just experienced and need a fresh perspective. What you're doing is taking the impact of an experience and smoothing it out using information. This is like getting auto-body work after a car accident. The car is not going to magically fix itself. You have to take it to the proper officials and they'll knock the dents out, replace whatever metal needs to be replaced, give you a new paint job (if necessary) and polish off your car's finish.

4. **Change your leadership beliefs:** A lot of creatives are disgusted with the thought of becoming leaders because they've seen so many negative, religious and broke folks in leadership. If this is the way you see leadership, you need to find some new people to look up to cause you're clearly looking at the wrong examples! I'm not telling you to leave your church! I'm telling you that it is okay to find positive examples of leadership to model yourself after! If you are going to

be an impactful leader, you have to change the way that you view leadership, otherwise, you'll pattern yourself after outdated models. Be an example of change. The next generation needs to see your version of what leadership looks like, not yesterday's model!

5. **Mature in your personal beliefs:** What you believe about yourself and others will affect your leadership. Your choices are directly tied to your self-view; your worldviews are tied to how you see yourself. Surround yourself with people who are not like you so that you won't be rigid and inflexible with your beliefs. It's okay to change your mind from time to time; it's okay to admit that you were wrong. This is maturity. We are all maturing in one way or another. If you think you're stupid or that no one values your leadership, get therapy. You have to be diligent and active in changing how you see yourself, because again, this will directly impact how you see and treat others.

6. **Change or expand your worldview:** Get out of this country sometime and go see the world at large! Don't limit yourself to your culture. Americans are some of the most prideful people because we don't get out much. The more you travel, the more your beliefs, plans and views will change. Read international news; find out what's going on in other countries. Ask yourself, "What can I do to change the world?" Be active in coming up with solutions, and if you're really bold, send your ideas to a businessman, a politician

or to a person who could consider or implement those ideas. Don't be afraid of rejection. Don't be afraid of being misunderstood. Just practice being the leader that you are. Some of your ideas won't be good; some of them may even get laughed at. But Reed Hastings and Marc Randolph pretty much got laughed at by Blockbuster. Today, Reed Hastings is worth $3.3 billion and Marc Randolph, who is no longer with Netflix, is worth $250 million. Who's laughing now?

7. **Form your belief system:** We talked about changing your thought-life, but a belief system is a little bit more complex. Think of it this way. Your thought-life is the way in which you see the world, your belief system is the foundation that you stand on to see the world. It determines your perspective. Your belief system is a series of beliefs that all come together to produce your perspective and your results. This is why you have to address the way that you think. If I told a young lady that she is beautiful, and I said this to her every single day, what I'm doing is altering her belief system. This is especially true if she's been told otherwise. She may have been told, for example, by her father that she's unattractive or, at minimum, led to believe that she's unattractive. I may serve as a father-figure in her life, so my job is to loosen the structure that her father built in her; her job is to pull it down. In other words, she has to work with me; I can't do all the work myself, otherwise, I run the risk of becoming her idol, and then, she may experience

what I call "false hurt." False hurt is when people feel like they've been rejected, misunderstood or mocked when, in truth, they simply started idolizing and depending on a leader for validation. When that leader failed to validate them as often as they think they should be validated, they convince themselves and others that they have been mishandled. This is false hurt. They weren't rejected or abused; they were just people with unrealistic expectations, so again, my job would be to dismantle the lies that her father told her. Her job is to pull down the structures and systems of beliefs that came as a result of those lies. There are a series of choices that she's made because of that one singular belief, so when she pulls down that belief, a lot of her other beliefs will become destabilized. They are all a part of her belief system. She then has to question and challenge those other beliefs, and if any of them are found to be faulty, dysfunctional or damaging, she has the responsibility of pulling them down. This is how you change your belief system.

8. **Become a valuable leader:** Earlier, I told you this—having a book means nothing, reading a book is nothing; a book's value is determined by what you extract from the book. The same is true for you. An organization can have a leader, but that leader's value within that organization is determined by what that organization is able to extract from that leader. You're not valuable to me if you have a bunch of ideas that I

have to implement; you become an asset when you implement or test your own ideas. You have to serve as an example. Martin Luther King, Jr. is valuable because he not only had a dream, but he shared it with the world. He brought people together, both Black and White, and he actively protested against racism in this country. He would not have been valuable if he'd chosen to stay at home and call another leader, talking about, "I have a dream." We all dream and we all have ideas about what it will take to make this world a better place. But only a handful of us are willing to get out and do something about our dreams; only a handful of us are willing to put on the big shoes of leadership and lead while we are still yet growing into those shoes and tripping over our own shadows.

9. **Embrace your big eyes (vision):** Sunglasses make us look cool, but they also dim our vision. Sometimes, we are so busy trying to be cool that we forget to be effective. Sometimes, we spend so much time trying to pacify the jealousy, the religiousness and the hatred of others that we fail to bring our full visions to fruition; this is because we fear upsetting others or, at minimum, getting their attention. But if we are going to be impactful, if we are going to change this world, we have to be willing to embrace our bigger-than-life visions at the expense of upsetting naysayers. Don't shrink your vision because of small-minded people. Remember, one percent of the wealth holders in this

world own over 50 percent of the world's wealth. They didn't get there by shrinking and apologizing for daring to be different; they didn't get there by conforming. They got there because they went up against the grain of society and made impactful changes to the world as we see it. They got there by being bold and unapologetic; they got there by taking risks that most of us are too afraid to take. Tyler Perry slept in his car! Let that sink in! He took his wages and put them all into a production; that production failed, and he ended up being homeless. He slept in a blue two-door 1992 Geo Metro until even that was repossessed. Can you imagine the number of people who called him crazy? Especially family members! Can you imagine the gossip that surrounded him? Nevertheless, he didn't allow all of the negativity to sway him. He had a dream; he had a huge vision, and he didn't apologize to anyone simply because they were too small-minded to see what he saw. It wasn't given to them to see. He had the sole responsibility of bringing his vision to pass. Don't minimize your vision; don't shrink it or dumb it down. Embrace it, even though it may be intimidating to you right now.

10. **The way up is down:** In other words, make humility a part of your daily diet. Many leaders have fallen into the pits of mediocrity because they got knowledge—that knowledge puffed them up and they refused to go to the gym to burn it off. What is the gym for leaders? Their knees! We humble ourselves on our knees, but

another weight that we have to be willing to carry is the burden and the blessing of accountability. It's not always easy to submit your great ideas to a leader, only to have him or her tell you that you're not ready to implement those ideas yet. This is especially true when you feel like you're ready and you're excited about your ideas, but being accountable keeps you from pushing out your ideas prematurely. Being accountable helps you to remain humble; this is what allows you to mature. When leaders are in the infancy of their leadership, they often fantasize about big platforms and seeing their names in spotlights. This is what we call ambition. Ambition can be both a blessing and a curse. It's a blessing if it's under control, but it can become a wildfire if it's not submitted to leadership. When uncontrolled ambition meets knowledge, it produces pride, and pride produces a pit for you to fall into. Stay humble. It's not an easy task, but holding yourself down when everything in you wants to rise up is the way that you beat your character into shape. This is how you become the unmovable, unshakable and powerful leader that you are set to become. This is how you overcome your first giant, which is yourself! Next, you don't have to deal with the demon of self-devaluation to be humble. Humility is not devaluing yourself. Humility is knowing how powerful and how valuable you are, but still being willing to roll your sleeves up and get your hands dirty.

11. **Innovate your leadership:** A lot of church and business boardrooms became war grounds every time two generations or more entered those boardrooms. For example, if a new and innovative pastor rises up in a church that's running on traditions from the forties and the fifties, that pastor is going to get some opposition. That pastor will know what warfare looks like by the time he leaves that boardroom. The same is true for a young and witty executive who dares to enter the boardroom of an organization that's still running on the old fumes of yesterday's creations. That executive will have to hold on to his or her wit; that executive will be ridiculed, mocked and threatened by the time the meeting is over. But look at what happened to Blockbuster. You can't afford to allow yourself to be bullied by yesterday's traditions and the people who uphold them. Be innovative; bring some fresh ideas to the table, but come to the table ready for war. Don't be emotional; be innovative. It's okay if your ideas are rejected. Sometimes, people have to keep running on fumes until they run out of ideas. When their old systems are no longer supporting them, they'll likely call you. Build, but don't be afraid to fail. I doubt if you'll ever find a successful leader who's never failed, but they didn't allow this to sway them. Come up with new ideas and implement them. Don't be afraid to dream, and be sure to dream big! Don't be afraid to pioneer new inventions or movements that have

never been seen before. You don't always have to enhance what's already in existence, it's okay to create something new. Innovate your leadership and don't apologize for doing so!

12. **Be a creative leader:** In other words, strategize; be a solutionist and not a complainer. Imagine being in a boardroom where everyone is screaming and complaining about the current condition of an organization or their opinions of what needs to be changed in order to keep the organization from going under. Despite how noisy it is, you sit there calmly, listening to everyone around you. You realize that many of them are saying the same thing in a different way or most of them have good ideas. You ask yourself in the midst of the chaos, "How do I marry all of their ideas together and create a solution?" You're unusually quiet. You pick up your pen and start scribbling down a few ideas. One of the leaders turn to you and shout, "You're awfully quiet over there! What do you recommend?" The boardroom suddenly quiets down as every head turns in your direction. You share what you've observed and you share your ideas. The meeting is adjourned and you're the hero! You didn't have to yell or belittle anyone. All you had to do was tap into your creative abilities while everyone around you was tapping into their emotions. A month later, you find yourself in another meeting. They want to give you a promotion and a huge raise. Why is this? Because you showed them how valuable

you are to their company. Of course, you can be valuable in your own company. You do this through self-discipline and by producing quality services, products or leaders; you do this by being innovative, humble and excellent. You do this by drowning out all of the noise around you, putting on your cape and changing the world. You are a super-hero in the making. Don't be afraid to soar like an eagle, even when most of the folks you see are on the ground like chickens, chasing each other around. Be creative, be bold,a and most of all, be yourself!

Remember, you aren't just creative, you are a creative. You are a force to be reckoned with. You are not just gifted, you are a gift and you have gifts (people) who add value to your life. It's your turn to make your mark on society and eventually, the world as a whole. Put away small talk (complaining, gossiping) and join the grown-up conversations. The world and everyone in it is waiting on you to take your place. The world and everyone in it is waiting on you to heal; we're all waiting on you to soar. Don't worry about everyone else around you. Be the greatest version of yourself that you can be. Don't allow people to fit you into their fears and convince you that it's God's will for you to be there. Break the mold of mediocrity. It's not for you to fit into. Break Cinderella's shoe. It's too small and too fragile for the journey up ahead of you. It's okay to be great; as a matter of fact, you were not placed on this Earth to be forgotten. Whatever it is that you're supposed to be building, start building it! And remember this, you don't just create the plan, you are the plan!

Homework (Activation)

Create a timeline of some of the events that have occurred in your life. Next, create a timeline projection of the accomplishments you plan to make over the next few years. Look at the example below.

- **1984:** Was born.
- **1995:** My parents divorced and my dad walked out of my life.
- **1997:** Started rebelling. Failed seventh grade.
- **1999:** Got pregnant with first child.
- **2004:** Had second child.
- **2007:** Started college.
- **2012:** Graduated college.
- **2015:** Got saved. Greatest day of my life!
- **2016:** Got married.
- **2018:** Got divorced. Almost lost my mind.
- **2020:** Started nonprofit organization for victims of abuse.

I also want you to create a timeline of your short-term goals. What are you planning to accomplish this year? Your short-term goals are whatever you plan to accomplish in the next three years. Make sure that you're reasonable. Don't just write something down. Think it through. Look at the example below.

- **2020:** Will go to therapy to work out some of the issues from my past. Will finish first book and launch my e-course.
- **2021:** Will get business license. Will also start looking at some properties for my business. Will write and publish second book.
- **2022:** Will launch brick and mortar company.

Also, break your short-term goals for this year down into months, for example:

2020:

- **June:** Will go to therapy.
- **September:** Finish and publish my first book.
- **December:** Launch my e-course.

By writing the vision and making it plain, you are more likely to fulfill it than you are to forget it. Activate your greatness; let's change the world!

Made in the USA
Columbia, SC
16 May 2020